ABC's of Selling

with

Etiquette

ABC's of Selling
with
Etiquette

by
DALE BRAKHAGE & EDIE HAND

Canterbury House Publishing

www.canterburyhousepublishing.com
Vilas, North Carolina

Canterbury House Publishing

225 Ira Harmon Road
Vilas, NC 28692
www.canterburyhousepublishing.com

Library of Congress Cataloging-in-Publication Data

Brakhage, Dale, 1956-
ABCs of selling with etiquette / by Dale Brakhage and Edie Hand.
p. cm.
ISBN 978-0-9825396-5-1
1. Selling--Social aspects. 2. Sales personnel--Attitudes.
3.Selling--Psychological aspects. I. Hand, Edie, 1951- II. Title.

HF5438.25.B696 2010
658.85--dc22

2010020975

Manufactured in the United States of America

First Printing September 2010

Contents

Contents (continued)

Dedication

Remember the very first time someone asked you to actually sell something? It was probably for a school fund-raiser. This book is dedicated to all students who, with no sales training whatsoever, have tried to sell candy bars, cookies, cleaning stuff, magazines, light bulbs or anything else for their school, band, scout troop or club.

It is also dedicated to all the parents, neighbors and friends who bought that stuff, not because they needed it, not because the students were good at selling, but because they love those students

It is especially dedicated to life's "persuaders," people who work in jobs where persuasiveness equals success: parents, teachers, preachers, politicians, lawyers, managers and especially salespeople.

Good selling!

Foreword

By Achievement Coach Greg Kilgore

Whether you are just starting-out in business or you are a seasoned sales professional, the format and straight-forward language of *ABCs of Selling with Etiquette* makes this book the ideal primer for a student of business or a budding sales associate, as well as, an efficient resource book and refresher for seasoned sales professionals. Likewise, sales managers and business education instructors can leverage the format, concise presentation of concepts, and basic language of the book for the professional development of call center teams, salesforces, and business classes.

What do you think of when you hear the terms "sales," "salesperson," and "selling?" As an Achievement Coach, I advise and coach people for professional productivity, business growth, and personal empowerment. As such, I have a lot of occasions to hear what people from all walks of life think about "selling" and "sales." More often than not, the value of the function of selling and the role of salespeople in our lives is misunderstood and often taken for granted.

In the *ABCs of Selling with Etiquette*, we will learn that selling is undeniably a function of communication necessary for every successful venture in industries, communities, national and international economies, civic life, and even personal relationships. A sales professional serves a vital role that is incalculably valuable and even a noble and honorable commitment to our way of life. You will come to realize that "selling" is presentation, organization, persuasion, and effectiveness that goes far beyond just trying to get others to buy products or services. As you read *ABCs of Selling with Etiquette*, you have an opportunity to re-discover the value and meaning of terms, such as, "selling," "sales," "salesperson," and "customer." Together we learn that "selling" is actually a form of communication not only between buyers and vendors, but also between professionals, colleagues, friends, and family.

Who do you know whose livelihood doesn't depend upon a salesperson in their company or organization to sell or promote a product or service to generate revenue? Do we not all endorse, even embrace, that living in a capitalist democracy requires productivity, production, sales, revenue, profits, and paychecks? The world continues to turn, so to speak, because many of us earnestly spend many hours of our lives in dedicated service to the provision of quality services or the production of quality goods for the benefit of our families, friends, neighbors, countrymen, and citizens of our global community. Each of us can acknowledge that there is not an aspect of your lifestyle that isn't a product or service that you purchased and were sold in order to sustain your quality of life... Products and services. Sales. Selling. Sold.

Not only does *ABCs of Selling with Etiquette* recommend essential "selling" strategies and methods for expressing yourself and your ideas, but *ABCs of Selling with Etiquette* also emphasizes a dimension of sales that is often neglected, the human-to-human conscientious courtesy of "business etiquette." Merging selling tactics and the practice of better human relations through business etiquette will help you learn to listen with intent and empathy, express and demonstrate respect for others with appropriate protocols and manners, better manage and present your ideas, work efficiently to achieve goals and objectives, communicate effectively, and ultimately create mutually-valuable and appreciated transactions of exchange between people.

The *ABCs of Selling with Etiquette* guides us to identify, practice, and adopt behaviors and to create habits that help us be effective in how we relate to others, our communications, and how we create value between people. Let's discover together that sales is not "someone trying to sell you something" or "you trying to get someone to buy your product." Rather, selling is genuine and authentic communication between people to create symbiotic relationships and achieve mutually-appreciated exchanges of value and satisfaction.

—Achievement Coach Greg Kilgore

Introduction:
How this book works for you

Selling touches everything around us. Can you see an object near you that has never been sold? Unless you made it yourself, probably not. We are all involved in buying and selling. Selling includes persuading others to accept you and choose your ideas. You constantly persuade other people to "buy" what you are "selling." The more persuasive you are, the more you get what you want out of life.

The purpose of this book is to de-mystify selling and improve your confidence when you sell. When you understand the essential concepts of how selling works, the mystery of selling disappears. If you take away the mystery, the stress of selling goes away. In every type of sale, certain events happen: An item or an idea is offered. When the seller and buyer agree on its value, then the buyer pays the seller and the buyer accepts ownership. From soup spoons to super computers, the essential concepts of selling apply.

This book assigns one concept of selling to each of the twenty-six letters of the English alphabet—a simple structure we know well and recall instantly. That makes the concepts easier to remember. You do not have to use all twenty-six concepts every time you want to sell something! Just as you choose the right few letters of the alphabet to spell different words, you choose the best few sales concepts to make different sales. Every selling situation is unique. Use only the sales concepts you need to make that sale.

The chapters of this book are short and easy to read. This book de-mystifies selling by explaining in simple language what selling is and how selling works. This book also presents essentials of etiquette which make up the professional behavior buyers expect from salespeople. Knowing how to act in selling situations increases your confidence, makes you more persuasive and helps you sell more.

If you start reading the book from chapter "A is for Ask," then the first time a concept appears in the book, it is in CAPITAL LETTERS to help you discover of the concepts of selling as you read along. For example, the concept, QUESTIONS, appears in that first chapter... You can turn immediately to the chapter "Q is for Questions" to learn about the concept. Feel free to skip around—learning about related concepts instead of reading chapters in order. What you want to learn (and when you want to learn it) is more important than the order of the chapters. Read the chapters in any order you like. The important thing is for you to learn.

This book moves quickly from topic to topic to prevent boredom. Like a sports car shifting gears in a race, the topics change quickly, moving you from sales to etiquette to insights and back to sales. The shifts are just enough to offer your brain a fresh re-start and a new perspective from section to section. Considering things from different perspectives helps you remember them.

These concepts are designed to be read and read again for review and reinforcement. Skills develop through practice and study. To receive the most benefit from the concepts in this book, read the concepts several times. Try using the concepts that make the most sense to you first. When you are comfortable using those, add another one. When you understand them, try using them in different combinations to see what works best for you. Work to fit one more concept into your selling every day. As you sell more, selling becomes fun. The more essential concepts you use, the more persuasive you will be. You sell more, you persuade others over to your way of thinking, you earn more money and you win recognition for your success. Get the essential concepts right, and all the rest falls into place. Watch your sales and your income grow as you become a skilled seller!

 is for Ask

"Ask and they will buy," versus, "Don't ask, don't sell."

Asking is an important part of every sale. Asking can be as simple as a gasoline pump flashing "Carwash? Yes or No" on a tiny video screen before it prints your receipt. On the other hand, asking can be as complicated as a contract hundreds of pages long used to sell the Navy a new aircraft carrier. In both cases, the seller asks, "Will you buy this?

Asking connects you to another person. Everyday, people pass right by you without making direct contact. When you ask someone a QUESTION, however, you make a connection. You capture that person's attention. For the moment, they focus on you. When you, as a seller, ask a buyer to give you something in exchange for whatever you are selling, you establish a link. Then it is up to that other person to answer your question. They can say YES or NO, or they can say maybe. They can even ignore you, but for a moment, you have their attention. They are now connected to you.

They are thinking about you because you asked them a question. It is that simple. When you ask someone a question, you connect. It does not matter if what you are selling is expensive or cheap. Your question can be ordinary such as "You want fries with that?" On the other hand, it may be life changing such as "Will you marry me?" Whatever you are asking, when you ask, they respond. Asking a question starts it all.

Asking is fundamental to selling. Do you agree that, if all else is equal, a salesperson who asks 10 CUSTOMERS to buy something will sell more than a salesperson who asks only five customers? Yes, they will, every time, because selling is a numbers game. Ask more; sell more. Not only is it important to ask many people, it is important to ask every customer you see to buy your product. It is easy to become involved in nice conversations with your customers and get distracted away from selling. Remember why you are there, to sell something, and remember to ask every customer to buy today. You sell more by asking more customers to buy whatever you are selling.

How you ask is important. Be polite. Be direct, and before you ask, make certain you give your customer a good reason to say yes. On the next page are three examples of how to ask a customer to buy something. The basic selling situation in this example is how most of us made our first sale, so it is an appropriate starting point.

Four elementary school students are selling candy bars door-to-door to raise money for their school. The first student just asks, "Do you WANT to buy a candy bar?" The second student says, "Hi. I am selling candy bars for my school. Would you please buy one from me today?" The third student says, "Mrs. Jones, my teacher at school really needs a new computer, and if we all sell 30 candy bars, we can buy her one right away. They are one dollar each. Would you like to buy two or three?" The fourth student sits at home and plays video games.

The first student will sell some candy bars if he asks enough neighbors. Most people do not sit around waiting to buy candy bars, but enough people like candy, so he will sell some. The second student will sell more than the first, because people who like candy will see a chance to help her school. She gave them a reason to buy. The third student will sell even more. He pleasantly and quickly explained why he is selling and what he is selling. He gives customers a chance to help him, his teacher and his school. They even get candy out of the deal! Did you notice that he asked them to buy MORE, two or three candy bars? He understands selling! Of course, the fourth student did not sell any because he did not try.

Before a customer will buy your product or SERVICE, they must understand what they are buying and what the PRICE will be. You present those details in a conversation before you ask them to buy.

It makes sense, does it not, to tell customers what the product and price are before you ask them to buy? Asking them to buy usually comes at the end. In a sales presentation, asking the customer to buy is "The Close." You "close" your selling presentation by asking them to buy. Look at these examples of questions you can use to ask customers to buy. They are quite different, but they all get to the same point, "Please buy."

- Would you like to buy this now?
- Would you prefer a red one or a blue one?
- Can I wrap this up for you?
- Will that be cash or credit card?

Some closing questions work better than others, but all of them work better than not asking. Put two salespeople on a street selling cookies. One of them just stands there saying nothing and the other asks everyone, "You wouldn't want to buy some of these today, would you?" The asker will sell more cookies, guaranteed. Since he asks a question, he connects with people. Some of them will buy his cookies, even if he is not asking as effectively as he possibly can.

At first, some people feel uncomfortable about selling. They feel uncomfortable asking directly of people to buy something. This is common and is more a fear of the unknown than a fear of selling. The unknown is what the customer is going to say. They may say yes, or they may say no. They may say maybe. You need to realize right now that saying yes, no or maybe is basically all they can do. So, what is there to be afraid of? Nothing, really.

Professional salespeople realize that more people are going to say "no" than "yes." (Realistically, if all customers said "yes" all the time, then there would be no need for salespeople! Every business would sell everything it could make. That never happens, so <u>salespeople will always have jobs</u>.)

The best salespeople know this. The more people they ask, the more often they will hear yes. They will also hear no many times, but that is okay. Salespeople understand that many people say no. That is just the way it goes in selling. When you are selling, remind yourself often that every "no, thank you," brings you closer to hearing the next "yes, I'll buy that." Train yourself to expect "yes" on every call. At the same time, do not allow the word "no" to disappoint you. Do not take "no" personally, it is simply part of the process of selling.

You can learn something from all your customers, the ones that buy and the ones who do not buy. After each sales call you make, take a moment to think about what happened. How did the customers react to what you said? As you evaluate your selling, you will discover that some words sell better than others do. Use them again. Experiment with the way you present your products and ask for the sale. As more customers say "yes" keep revising your questions to make them more effective.

Note: There is a big difference between selling and order-taking. For example, when you bring your groceries to the checkout line in a grocery store, the grocery clerk does not ask you if you want to purchase. She understands that you want to pay the marked price for those goods. Order-taking is simply taking money from customers that have already decided to buy. Salespeople can certainly take an order, but that is not really selling. Selling is persuading others to buy from you. The following 25 chapters in this book contain other essential concepts of selling that will make you more persuasive and better at selling.

Etiquette Essentials
The Value of Etiquette and Greetings

As you read before, what makes many people uncomfortable about selling is the fear of the unknown. That is a very common feeling! Not knowing what will happen next makes most people uncomfortable. That is why society invented etiquette. Etiquette, or manners, is a set of expectations that most people share in given situations. Etiquette makes people feel comfortable around new people in new situations. When you "mind your manners" you are making other people around you feel more comfortable. When that happens, they are much more likely to buy from you. You are much more likely to persuade them to your way of thinking.

An essential of etiquette, is how you greet people... How you address people the very first time each day, sets the tone for the rest of your discussions. If they know you well or if they have never met you, it is up to you to make them feel comfortable with you. Use the following steps to greet people, and they will want to listen to you.

First, always be pleasant. Before the other person can hear you or see you, make a conscious decision to project your best image. Here is how to do that: Take a deep breath to calm yourself, put a smile on your face, stand up straight and think to yourself, "This conversation is going to go well." This only takes half a second, but it is very important. If you appear nervous or negative to the other person, they will immediately put up defenses before they listen to you.

Respect a person's personal space. We each have a "comfort zone" of space around ourselves, and it is different for each person. If you walk up too close to anyone the first time you meet them, then they will feel uncomfortable and back away. They will not want to talk to you. Stay at least an arm's length away, and watch them carefully to see how close they want you to be. If they are interested in what you are saying, they can move closer to you if they want.

Be friendly. The old saying goes, "If you want to have friends, be a friend." Smile and say something friendly like, "Good morning," or "Hello, thank you for meeting with me." Speak directly to the person and look right into their eyes as you speak.

Speak respectfully. Leave out any slang or trendy expressions like: "What's up?" "How ya doin'?" "Mornin." "Hey, Man." Addressing people formally is a sign of respect. It shows them that you are being serious about talking with them. In business, unless you already know someone very well, address the person using a title. Use "mister," "misses," "miss," "doctor," etc., in front of the last name.

Here are some examples:

"Hello, Mister Baker."
"Good morning, Misses Strong."
"Nice to meet you, Doctor Taylor."

One of the most comforting sounds we can hear is our own name. If you know the other person's name and know how to pronounce it correctly, then say their name. It makes people feel comfortable around you. If you are not sure how to pronounce their name correctly, then just use a greeting like those above.

You may not be accustomed to using formal greetings. For a while, they were going out of style, but now they are making a classy comeback. Using them sets you apart from the crowd and shows the other person you are a respectful, serious person. Addressing someone properly takes only a moment, but it is very important. In a very short time, you make the other person feel comfortable about you. You seem pleasant, respectful and friendly to them, so they will probably listen to what you have to say next.

When you address people that you already know, use the same technique, but use their first name. People will tell you when it is okay to use their first name. That is a good sign that you have established a relationship with that person and that they are beginning to trust you.

A Different Perspective: Selling Happens Everywhere!

Professional salespeople earn their living by selling their company's products. Politicians win elections by selling the public on voting for them. Religious leaders grow their groups by selling people on believing in a particular way. Single people get dates by selling other people on the idea of going out with them. When two people like each other enough, they sell each other on the idea of getting married. Parents sell their ideas of how to live a happy and productive life to their children. Friends go to a particular movie or restaurant after someone in the group sells the others on the idea. As you can see, "selling" goes on all the time. In fact, you have been selling all your life, even if you did not realize it. Everyone sells!

Anytime you try to persuade another person that you have a valuable idea, you are selling. That is much different from the picture in most people's minds when you mention selling: A slick, pushy, fast talking salesman in a plaid sports coat trying to sell beat up cars to anybody who happens to walk by his used car lot! Only a small percentage of people sell products professionally. Most people "sell" every day as amateurs. They are the ones persuading students, friends, voters, congregations, children, etc., to believe in the VALUE of their ideas.

For those of you who are already professional salespeople, this book is a quick-and-easy-review of the essential behaviors that make sales happen. Professional salespeople know that a regular review of the essentials can keep their selling skills sharp. Since you have not seen the essentials presented in this format before, this unique presentation will be an interesting review for you.

If you are like most people, this book will open your eyes to how selling works and show you how to be more persuasive. Most people can see big positive changes in their lives from applying these essential concepts. Please recommend this book to as many of those people as you can. They will thank you for it. Now it is time to learn another concept!

 is for Benefits

Facts tell. Benefits sell.

Facts are what your product is. Benefits are what other people believe your product does for them. Benefits are much stronger in selling than facts. Why is that true? Because people buy things after they believe in the benefits, not before. The moment people believe that something, anything, will provide a benefit for them, they begin to want it. When they want something enough, they buy it. Facts tell; benefits sell.

We buy things for what the product can do for us. We buy light bulbs for the benefit of seeing after dark. We buy trashcans for the benefit of not having stinky trash all over our house. We buy coffee for the benefit of waking up and feeling alert. We buy insurance for the benefit of feeling secure about the future.

We buy gasoline, not because of these facts: It is poisonous, smells terrible and can easily explode, but because of this benefit: It fuels our cars so we have the freedom to travel wherever and whenever we want to go! The facts about gasoline do not make anyone want to buy it. It is the benefit gasoline provides that makes us buy it. We will keep buying it, even though the price goes higher and higher, until there is some other convenient way for us to travel.

Here is a comparison of facts and benefits: Consider a cell phone...

Facts	Benefits
It is small.	You can carry it with you easily and stay in touch.
It is plastic.	It is tough. Drop it, and it will not break like glass.
It has numbers.	You can talk to the world by pushing the numbers.
It has a battery.	You are free to use it anywhere you want to go.
It stores data.	Important phone numbers are always there for you.

Do you see the difference between facts and benefits? Facts just tell about something. Facts are all about your product. Benefits, on the other hand, are all about your customer. Benefits show how your customer's life will be better! When you are the customer buying a product, are you interested in it, or what it will do for you?

To discover the benefits of your product or service, state a fact about it and then ask, "So what does this do to help the customer?" An even easier way is to ask, "So what?" In the cell phone example above, the first fact was, "It is small." So what? You can carry it with you easily and stay in touch with your friends, family, co-workers, etc. As you can see, a benefit answers the "So what?" for a fact. Remember, a benefit explains to customers what the product does for them.

To sell anything as quickly as possible, always describe the benefits to your customer. Put yourself in your buyer's place for a moment, JOIN their world and imagine what challenges that customer must face. Ask them what they want the product to do for them. They will tell you. That is your chance to explain to the customer how your product's benefits match what the customer just said. As you describe the benefits, describe how your product helps the customer solve problems and be happier. When you are talking about benefits, you are talking about your customer instead of your product. It is all about them. Customers will appreciate your help.

To be more persuasive, always follow a fact with a benefit. Explain what good things the product will do. If your customer agrees, they will want to buy your product. A thousand facts might not make a customer want to buy your product. One good benefit will.

Here is an example of selling with benefits: A customer just entered a cell phone store and was greeted by a salesperson. The customer said he wanted to buy a new cell phone. Some salespeople would immediately start showing the customer different phones. The smart salesperson, however, will focus on the customer first. She will talk more about the customer then cell phones. She asks the customer, "What did your old phone do for you that you really liked?"

In this case, the customer says he likes how he can talk a long time without recharging the battery, and he likes how he can make calls from almost anywhere. Those are two important benefits; so any new phone the salesperson shows should have a long-lasting battery and great reception.

Then the salesperson asks, "Is there anything you'd like your new phone to do that your old phone couldn't?" The customer replies, "Yes, I like to check my e-mail from my new phone."

By asking two short questions, the smart salesperson has learned important benefits that the customer wants in a new phone. Right away, she can show the customer several models that provide those benefits. The customer is glad the salesperson is not wasting his time, and he is much more likely to buy a phone that can do the things he wants.

Etiquette Essentials

Business Cards

Everyone in business should have their own business cards. That is a fact. We will get to the benefits of business cards in a moment. A business card is about three inches wide and two inches tall. Printed on one side of the card are your name, your title (what you do), your organization and how you can be reached. The best business cards are simple and designed to remind people about you. Businesspeople keep files of business cards from people that they may want to do business with in the future. A file of business cards serves the same purpose as your e-mail contacts list. It represents people you have met in person. Keep other people's cards in alphabetical order as you collect them to find them quickly later.

It is good business manners to take your business cards with you all the time. When you meet a new person with whom you are doing business for the first time, hand the person one of your cards. Say, "Here is my card. May I have one of yours?" Most business people are happy to exchange cards with you. They now have your contact information. That is a fact. So what? A benefit of giving them your business card is this: You have just made it easy for them to contact you when they are ready to do business.

It is also good business manners to leave one of your cards behind if you attempt to visit someone who is away or unavailable. Give your card to the secretary or receptionist and ask them to please give it to the person you came to see. You just made it easy for that receptionist to pass your information along. Some people call business cards "calling cards" for just that reason.

Most people consider it poor manners to write notes on your business cards. If you want to leave someone a note, write it on a separate piece of paper and attach it to your business card with a paper clip. You should never write notes on someone else's card while you are meeting with them. After your meeting, when they are gone, you can make notes on their card if you like. For example, always write the date you met with that person. That can be a very useful piece of information for you. Believe it or not, it is easy for weeks and months to go by without calling someone you intended to get back to right away.

Some businesses provide elaborate cards for their employees. These cards have color photographs and a company logo (their identifying symbol). Some even have products printed on the back. They want their card to grab attention. That is fine, but most business cards are straight-forward and simple with a blank back.

Having business cards, and knowing how and when to use them are signs of a professional businessperson. If you are a student, it is perfectly acceptable to have business cards made with your name, your school, and your contact information. For your title, print "Student."

Business cards provide a benefit to everyone you meet. Those people can now easily remember you and contact you in the future. In business, it is often not who you know but who knows you, that brings you opportunities for success. Make it easy for people to remember you with business cards!

When trying to be helpful, focus on the little things.

– Edie Hand

is for Customers

Selling would be so easy if we could do it without all those customers!

Successful selling is all about customers. Here is the most important point about selling. The product you want to sell is not the most important thing. The most important thing is what your customers want your product to do for them. When they believe your product has benefits for them, they will buy it.

Where do you find customers? They are everywhere. To find your customers, just put yourself in their place. For example, if you are selling jewelry, think to yourself, "Where would I be if I wanted to buy jewelry?" The answer is obvious, in a jewelry store. To sell jewelry, you set up a jewelry store. If you are selling hot dogs, you can find hungry customers at baseball parks, city corners at lunchtime, etc. If you are selling the latest incredible kitchen gadget, you can find millions of customers watching their TVs late at night, so run a TV infomercial. If you are selling candy for your school organization, your customers are your friends and neighbors in your neighborhood.

Your next question is, "How would I want to be treated if I were a customer?" The answer to that question is a little tougher. Not all customers want to be treated the same, but they all want friendly service. They all want to be appreciated, and they all want to receive respect. They absolutely all want fairness and HONESTY, and they all want to get the best value for their money.

All sales begin at the beginning with the FIRST IMPRESSION. Salespeople have three seconds to make a positive first impression. Three seconds is all it takes for a customer to decide whether or not they like you. To create a good first impression, have a neat appearance and smile! Greet customers with ENTHUSIASM and warmth. The customer will glance at you and make an immediate judgment based on your appearance and your attitude (your apparent desire to be of service). This immediate judgment by customers is the best reason salespeople should always dress for success. Always wear your nicest clothes and your best attitude to work.

The best salespeople immediately greet customers in a friendly manner and, at the same time, evaluate every customer's response to the greeting. You can see right away whether or not a customer wants personal attention. Pay attention to the customer's body language. If this new customer moves toward you and begins a conversation with you, it is safe to stay closer. If the customer moves away from you with a gesture or an unresponsive reply, it is better for you to give them their space. Be ready to assist that customer when they indicate they want your help.

No two customers act alike. You can never predict how a customer will act by their appearance. You cannot judge a book by its cover, and you cannot judge a customer by their clothes. Today, millionaires dress like homeless people, and homeless people dress like millionaires. It is a big mistake to assume how much someone can pay by how they dress. Instead, treat all new customers the same. Try to sell everyone until it is clear they cannot afford your product. This is also true when you are selling to businesses. In tough economic times, many businesses look fine from the street, but they are broke. Never underestimate their ability to buy, but never deliver the product until you have done a credit check or received your payment in advance!

Without customers, there would be no sales. Everything salespeople say or do should focus on what the customer wants. Incredibly, however, many salespeople focus on themselves! They are more concerned with selling their product than they are with what customers want. These salespeople focus on what they think about the customer rather than what the customer thinks about them. Customers do not respect these "pushy" salespeople. Self-centered salespeople sell less than "customer-oriented" salespeople do. Customers want you to care more about them and less about yourself.

We started this chapter with the most important point in selling. The most important thing in selling is *not* your product, it is what the customer wants your product to do for them! Before you say anything or show any product to a customer, think to yourself, "What does this customer want?" Obviously, if you do not know what that customer wants, you need to ask. In the chapter on questions, you will find tips on exactly how to ask a customer what they want. Once you know what the customer wants, you can share the product's benefits that match the customer's wants.

It takes much more work to gain a new customer than it does to keep an old customer. Old customers, regular customers and repeat customers, are the foundation of any business. On the average, 80% of any business comes from 20% of the customers. That is the 80/20 Rule of sales, and it highlights how important repeat customers are for you.

Repeat customers should be treated with more attention and faster response than new customers. Be careful! Sometimes it is easy to take your repeat customers for granted. Do not let that happen. Remember, other salespeople are doing their best to turn your repeat customers into their new customers!

Here is one last thing about customers. Everyone agrees that people who trade their money for your product are customers. Life, however, is about so much more than that! Everyone is a customer.

Everyone has something to give you, and you should treat everyone like a customer. Your parents and your children have respect they can give you, or not; treat them like customers. Your spouse has love he/she can give you, or not; treat your spouse like a customer. Your co-workers have help and support they can provide you, or not; better treat them like customers! Your mail carrier, your barber, your garbage man, waiters in restaurants, etc., can all provide you with excellent service, or not; treat them as you would a customer to get great service. Even your pets can give you love and attention, or not. Please be certain to treat your pets like customers! How much better would this world be if all its leaders treated their people and other countries like customers?

Etiquette Essentials

Conversation

To be persuasive and good at sales you need to be good at conversation. A conversation is an exchange of information between two people. Do you remember the most important thing about selling? The same principle applies to conversation. The most important thing in a conversation is not what you have to say, it is what the other person says and what he/she believes about what you said. Follow these simple skills, and people will want to have conversations with you, and they will tend to believe what you say.

When you have a conversation with someone, make them the focus of your universe. Concentrate your attention on them. Look at them. Look them right in the eyes. You can tell a lot about what a person is saying from watching their eyes. If you are watching their eyes, they can watch yours too. They can see that you are paying complete attention to what they have to say. That makes people comfortable sharing information with you.

People who do not want to make eye contact with you may be uncomfortable with what they have to say or with what you are telling them. They may be hiding something. Consider that as you do business with that person. Some people simply have a poor habit of not looking at other people during conversations. That is perfectly fine for them, but you will be more persuasive when you share eye contact. They will know you are not hiding anything from them. When people are comfortable sharing information with you, they become comfortable believing what you share with them. That makes you more persuasive.

Let people talk! Of course, you can think faster than you can talk. Everyone can. During a conversation, you will have all kinds of thoughts about what the other person is saying. You may be tempted to interrupt the other person in order to persuade them to your way of thinking. Do not interrupt! If you begin speaking before another person finishes a sentence, you appear pushy, rude and selfish. The other person will immediately think you care more about what you are trying to sell than what they want to buy. They will put up defenses, and you will probably lose the sale. Wait for others to finish their sentences.

A very useful conversation tool is the "pause." Train yourself to pause briefly after the other person has spoken. That short pause will allow time for you to consider what they said. It will make you appear thoughtful and considerate. When the other person in the conversation is comfortable that you are listening to what they have to say, he/she will be more comfortable listening to and believing in what you say. Being a better listener makes you more persuasive.

Be careful to control your facial expressions during conversations. Smiling politely is the best expression. Not a huge grin, just a small smile, encourages people to talk. If you frown, or shake your head as people tell you something, you might as well be interrupting their sentence by shouting, "No!" The result is the same. They will stop sharing information with you, and they will become defensive. That ends a conversation. Try instead to keep a neutral "poker face" expression when people are disagreeing with you. Take an interest in what they are saying rather than taking a position. Be as neutral as you can. Then the conversation can go on.

Conversations are the keys that unlock sales. Exchanging information with customers allows you to learn what they want and encourage them to buy your product. A good conversation can turn a customer's "no" into "yes." Good questions make better conversations. You will learn how this works when you read the chapter Q is for Questions.

It is also important to remember common courtesy: Saying "please" and "thank you," letting other people go first in lines, opening doors for other people, using good manners, smiling and being pleasant. Professionalism is how you perform your job. Courtesy is how you perform your humanity. If you are good at your job, you will be rewarded with pay and benefits. If you are courteous to other people, you will be rewarded with their respect and cooperation. You will be more persuasive.

Remember The Golden Rule: Do unto others as you would have them do unto you.

– Edie Hand

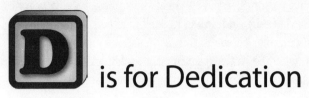 is for Dedication

The suitcase of success!

At any busy airport, you will see business people hurrying to their destinations pulling a small black suitcase on wheels. Those portable suitcases all have tiny wheels and pull-out handles. They are small, but they have extra pockets and zippers so a person can carry everything he/she needs on a trip. Experienced businesspeople learn how to pack those suitcases with exactly the things they need. There is no room for anything extra. Dedication is like those small black suitcases on wheels.

Dedication helps you focus on the things you need on your trip to success. Dedication teaches you to leave behind the extra things you do not really need. Once you learn how to use it, dedication makes your journey to success much easier. So, how does dedication work and how do you learn to use it?

Dedication is focusing your thoughts and actions to accomplish something. Actions are a tremendously important part of dedication. Focusing your thoughts points your attention in the right direction. Then taking action accomplishes things. Focused thinking is only a first step. You must take action to make sales happen!

People who win awards for great accomplishments always receive great praise for their dedication. It does not matter how long it took to accomplish the deed. For example, a retiree receiving a gold watch for 20 years of service and a soldier receiving a medal for one hour of extreme bravery in battle both receive praise for their dedication. The common thread in both examples is focused, persistent and perhaps unwavering attention and action. Their focus became actions that accomplished great things.

How does dedication work? First, you choose to be successful. That is a choice you must make consciously like deciding to go on a trip. Second, you must decide what actions you must perform to be successful. Third, you focus on those actions, and you get them done. If you succeed the first time, that is great! If you do not succeed, then you try again. You keep trying until you accomplish what you decided to do. That is persistence. Persistence overcomes obstacles. The best example of persistence is the Grand Canyon. For hundreds of centuries, water persistently flowing through the canyon washed away the rock and dug what is now one of the wonders of the natural world.

Persistence is a part of dedication. Persistence is one of the most powerful tools of life. It comes with a 100% guarantee. If you persist in taking the actions required to accomplish your GOAL, if you do not quit, then you have a 100% better chance of accomplishing your goal than anyone who quits. Persistence pays!

When you focus on only the actions you must take to succeed and you avoid activities that will not help you reach your goal, then you are dedicated. You spend your valuable time doing the things that will get you closer to your desired result. Dedication helps you succeed faster than other people who get distracted by other activities. Dedication helps you focus on the things you need to succeed, and it helps you leave unimportant things behind you. Just like one of those small black airport suitcases, dedication helps you move swiftly and easily toward where you want to be in your life.

Etiquette Essentials
Dependability

To be dependable, do things correctly and on time. In school, teachers depend on their students to show up for class and to complete their assignments. In business, customers expect salespeople to be at work on time and to provide good service. Generally in life, friends and family depend on you to do the things that you say you will do. The bottom line of being dependable is this: If you tell someone you will do something, do it. That is called being true to your word.

How do you feel when someone lets you down? Are you disappointed? Are you angry? You probably are not ready to place your trust in that person again soon. That is the way people will feel about you if you are not dependable.

So many people today seem unreliable. That is why we do not trust strangers. This means it is up to you, the salesperson, to earn the trust of each customer by being dependable. Each customer you work with will constantly judge your actions. Did you do all the things you promised? Did you deliver what you promised on time? Is that product you sold them as good as you said? Did it do what you said it would do? Customers ask these questions about you every time they buy. If the answers are all yes, you are dependable. When your customers learn that they can depend upon you, the bonus is that they will tell their friends to buy from you too. If the answer to just one of those questions is no, then you are not dependable, and they will tell even more friends to stay away from you. Unfortunately, people love to spread bad news about undependable people.

The very same circumstances apply to friends and family. Everyone enjoys being around friends and family members who are dependable. If you are not, people will avoid you. No matter what the commitments, you should always deliver whatever you promise.

A good saying to live by is: "Always under-promise and over-deliver." Do more than you say you will do. Do things earlier than people expect you to do them. You will soon have a reputation for being dependable. Customers will come back to you to buy more, and you will have more friends.

A Different Perspective: Why did Dale write this book?

I love building things. When I was in middle school, I built model cars. As a teenager, I discovered real cars! There is nothing better than taking something apart to figure out how it works, and then making it work better. (Or making it go faster! Like with cars!)

When I earned a degree in Educational Psychology, I enjoyed studying how learning works. I learned how people can change their behavior to make their lives work better. Later, as I began my career in sales, I applied psychology to my work in sales. Immediately, I observed differences in the behavior of the award-winning salespeople and the other salespeople.

It was relatively simple to adopt those award-winning behaviors and succeed in sales.

After over 30 years of successful selling, managing and training, I wanted a new challenge. Our two children were off in college, and I had time to tackle something new like searching for and discovering the secret to selling anything! That would be a great accomplishment. I decided to go for it.

First, I used my training in educational psychology to analyze the complex process of selling to discover exactly how selling works. I took selling apart and broke it down into its essential concepts.

Working at night and on weekends, I did it. I thought it might take a week or two, but it took several years. I had no idea how difficult it could be to analyze and organize everything we simply call "selling." But I was dedicated to the project, so I had to finish it!

In any case, when I finished I had the secret to selling anything, the essential concepts of selling! That was a fact. So what? Could I explain the concepts in a simple way so anyone could learn to apply them and sell better? Absolutely. I just needed to organize my findings into a system everyone could identify with like the alphabet! More nights and weekends later, and here it is! I hope you like it.

Mental toughness is essential to success.

– Vince Lombardi, Hall of Fame Coach
of the NFL Champion Green Bay Packers

is for Enthusiasm!

Yes indeed, enthusiasm sells!

Enthusiasm is the energy of a positive attitude overflowing out of a person. You can see enthusiasm in how a person sits, stands, walks and talks. You can see enthusiasm in the expression on their face, and in how many hours they work each day. You can spot an enthusiastic person a mile away. Whenever people are obviously positive about something, we call them enthusiastic.

The most important thing about enthusiasm in selling is this: Enthusiasm is contagious! You can catch enthusiasm two ways: From other people; and from your dreams. Enthusiastic people infect others with their positive energy. It flows from their smiling faces, their energetic talk and their obvious passion for their cause. If they have a great product, that is good. Even if they have a poor product, enthusiasm itself can make customers take notice.

Customers will respond well to your positive enthusiasm (as long as you do not overwhelm them with it). Customers will overlook small flaws in your sales presentation if you are selling with enthusiasm. Your positive energy is the key to their acceptance. Most people are attracted to positive energy from another person. As you would expect, most people avoid others who are acting negatively. This is the most important reason why salespeople need to keep a positive attitude. Your positive attitude expresses itself as enthusiasm, and that enthusiasm attracts customers who will catch your enthusiasm for your product.

How do you develop enthusiasm? First, catch it from others. Hang out with enthusiastic people and avoid negative people. Read books written by enthusiastic authors. Watch enthusiastic people on TV, and open yourself up to their positive attitudes. Second, catch enthusiasm from your dreams.

Think about your dream of success. Imagine yourself as successful. See your success in your mind and feel how good it will be. The positive power of your dreams and imagination will fuel your enthusiasm.

Have you ever worked extra hard to win a prize? Have you ever saved money to buy some special something? Having a dream is the same principle, but on a grander scale. You may dream about owning a certain type of car, you may dream of a trip to an exotic country, or you may dream of a new house! Dreams like that can motivate you to keep working when jobs are hard or when times are tough. Find pictures of your dream thing and put them in places where you can see them. They can remind you that one day your hard work will turn your dream into a reality.

It takes a while to build enthusiasm. You should not expect to become truly enthusiastic overnight. It takes practice. You can act enthusiastically any time you choose. You can decide at any moment to think positively or negatively about any situation. When you choose to be positive, you will find it easier to be enthusiastic. The positive power spilling out of an enthusiastic person comes from their positive thoughts. Here is how it works…

First, focus your mind on positive thoughts such as:

- This is a good product.
- This product will sell.
- Customers will buy from me today.
- I will be successful in this job.

Second, reject any negative thoughts such as:

- This will not work.
- No way I can sell this.
- Nobody is going to buy this.

Since you can only think one thought at a time, you can train your brain to think positively. When negative thoughts start (and they will—everybody gets negative thoughts), immediately tell yourself to forget that. Say it aloud to emphasize the point. (If you are not alone, be ready to explain that you are building enthusiasm, otherwise people might think you are a little crazy!) Then, deliberately replace that negative thought with a positive one. It is just like writing, when you erase a mistake and rewrite it correctly. Here is an example: You are driving home from work, and the negative thought pops into your head that another car might crash into you. Immediately, recognize that idea as a negative thought. Then, deliberately think to yourself, "Forget that!" Then consciously replace that negative thought with the mental picture of you safely arriving at home.

If a negative thought like, "He is not going to buy this," pops into your head before you see a customer, erase it! Forget that thought and replace it with a thought of the customer saying, "Yes."

After a while, maybe weeks or months, you will be so aware of positive and negative thinking that you will nearly always think positively. In time, thinking positively will become a great habit and a forceful tool for better living. When your brain is full of positive thoughts, energy from those thoughts spills out in the form of enthusiastic actions. You smile, and you speak with friendliness and confidence. You feel better too. Your body language confirms to your customers that you know what you are talking about here. Your customers notice your positive energy, and that is when they catch your enthusiasm!

Here is one word about trying to fake it. Stop. If you have truly negative thoughts about what you are selling, then stop. Customers will avoid your bad attitude and false enthusiasm. To get back on track with genuine enthusiasm, take some time to think positive thoughts about what you are selling. Get help from other enthusiastic people. Learn what they think to get positive and enthusiastic about the product. Find something to be enthusiastic about, and then you can genuinely become enthusiastic.

As you work to become more positive and enthusiastic, your sales results will improve. Your success will make you even more enthusiastic. How powerful is enthusiasm? Consider this. People who have all the physical, mental and spiritual tools to win can fail without enthusiasm. On the other hand, people with very few tools for success will succeed if they enthusiastically keep trying. What's more, others will catch that enthusiasm and help them succeed.

By the way, do you remember that customers include your family, coworkers, friends and neighbors? They will also enjoy your enthusiasm. Positive, enthusiastic people are fun to be near. Of course, this means you will need to become positive and enthusiastic about all aspects of your life. Go ahead! You will be a happier healthier person for it.

Etiquette Essentials

Empathy

A second-cousin to enthusiasm is empathy. Empathy is the ability to share someone else's feelings. Some people are naturally good at empathy. Others must work at it. How does empathy work? Watch people carefully. Watching others' appearance and actions will give you clues about how they feel. Here are some basic examples: Happy people smile. Angry people frown. Excited people talk quickly with enthusiasm. Bored people do not talk very much, and they look around the room. Interested people look right at you and engage in conversation with you.

An old saying is, "The eyes are the window to the soul." You can learn a lot about how another person is feeling by studying their eyes. People's eyes show happiness, anger, curiosity, humor, and almost all the other emotions. After you read this, try this simple exercise: Go watch television for a while with the sound turned off. Pay particular attention to the actors' eyes. You will be able to tell how they are feeling.

In real life, it is easy to empathize with people. Most people display very easy-to-read signs about their emotions. Practice reading those signs and you will get better at it soon. People with empathy are naturally more persuasive because they can judge how other people are feeling about the conversation. When your goal is to persuade another person to believe in the value of your ideas, good empathy skills allow you to gauge your progress. You will be able to see if the customer does not believe you as well as when they gain interest in your presentation. You will also be able to see if the customer begins to get bored or restless with you. By watching your customer carefully with empathy, you can quickly see what is happening, and you can change the direction of the conversation to something more interesting.

Have empathy. Pay close attention to how people around you feel about what you are saying. Then you can make small adjustments to your presentation based on their responses, and persuade them to your way of thinking much more quickly!

We cannot control life's events but we can manage how we respond to them.

– Edie Hand

is for First Impression

Meet the 3-second sale.

You have three seconds or less to make a good first impression with customers. It does not matter if they are seeing you in person, listening to you on the phone, or reading your letter or e-mail message. They decide to like you or not in the first three seconds.

If you make a good first impression, the customer is more likely to listen to what you have to say. So what makes a good first impression? A professional image works best. Two things are very important for your professional image: your overall appearance and your smile.

Your overall appearance includes your grooming, posture and clothing. You should always appear clean and well-groomed. Stand up straight, and sit with good posture. When you appear healthy, happy and alert, you impress others—especially other business professionals.

To select what clothing to wear, let your surroundings tell you what will fit in the best. If you are calling on professionals in office buildings, a business suit will work. If you are calling on industrial workers in shops, slacks and a golf shirt will project the right image. If you are selling for a charity group and have a uniform, wear it proudly and correctly. Successful salespeople learn that they can fit in with their customers and project a professional image at the same time.

Customers make their first impression based upon how well you fit into their idea of what a good salesperson should look like, sound like or write like. First impressions are really not about you. First impressions are actually about how your customers perceive you.

If that is true, how can any salesperson guess what every single one of their customers wants to see and hear? You win by playing the odds.

Salespeople know what most customers want to see. They want to see a smiling, clean, well-groomed and professional salesperson. Customers look for someone who genuinely cares more about what they want to buy than what salespeople want to sell. All customers want a salesperson that makes the extra effort to present themselves in the best possible light.

Customers form a new first impression of you every time they see you. Even if you have established a friendship with the customers, they still assess you every time they see you. They decide immediately if they are going to spend time listening to you that day, so it is very important for you to make a good first impression each time you meet someone.

So how exactly do you make a good first impression? Inside sales people working in stores make a good first impression by letting customers identify them easily. Wear your uniform or name badge proudly. Pay attention to the customers. Smile at them and speak as soon as you see them. Let them know you are prepared to help them whenever they are ready for help. The absolute worst thing you can do as an inside sales person is ignore a customer. Customers are more likely to buy a product if they know you are ready and willing to help them when they need you. On the other hand, if customers feel like you cannot be bothered to help them, they will go somewhere else. They will find another store and a more attentive salesperson to take their money.

If you are an outside sales person, you travel to see your customers. The most important thing for you to remember about first impressions is this: Be ready. You often have to wait to see the decision maker. Know when your customer will first be able to see you or hear you. You do not want to appear distracted or daydreaming when the customer appears. That projects a first impression of, "I'm not ready."

Customers want to do business with salespeople who are always ready to help them. So be on the lookout. If you are waiting outside a door, stay alert to hear the customer coming. If you are in a waiting room, be ready when they call you. If you are waiting in the customer's office, stay alert to hear the customer coming.

When your customer can see you, speak up with a smile and a friendly greeting. Say their name if you know how to pronounce it correctly. Everyone is attracted to the sound of his or her name. Congratulations! You just made a positive first impression, and you are on your way to making your sale.

A Different Perspective: Oh, no! Someone expects YOU to sell!

If you are reading this book, you have probably felt this way. There is a natural sense of stress and fear that comes with a sales goal no matter if your goal is to sell a box of cookies or a million dollars of real estate. That stress comes from the fear of three unknowns:

- Who is going to buy it?
- How am I going to sell it?
- When will they buy?

That stress is normal. Everyone feels it. The good news is this: You can reduce stress by eliminating the unknowns.

Successful salespeople work with very little stress. They know and understand the essential concepts of selling, so they already know the answers to two of the three questions above. They were not born with that KNOWLEDGE. They learned it through training and years of experience. When professional salespeople go to work, they know who is likely to buy and how they are going to sell. With the knowledge that comes from understanding and using the essential sales concepts from this book in every sales situation, effective salespeople have eliminated at least two of the three unknowns. The only remaining unknown to handle during the sales process is: When will the customer buy?

Unknowns can make anyone feel uncomfortable, and no one likes rejection. To overcome the fear that comes from unknowns and the possibility of rejection, you need to understand how fear works. How does fear work? Our brain analyzes our current situation, searches memories for similar experiences, compares the two, and then uses our imagination to picture an outcome. If an imagined outcome is unpleasant, then fear increases the stress you feel by degree until it stops you and you get out of the current situation. The greater your imagination, the stronger your fear and stress can be. It begins by plaguing you with small doubts, and then it can increase and cause you to imagine terrible things. The result is that you procrastinate putting off doing the task that frightens you. If you put off making the sales call, then you do not make the sale.

Here is how you overcome fear: You face it and recognize fear for what it is—a thought process. The key to overcoming fear is realizing that fear is merely a thought process in which you can only focus on one thought at a time and you can choose what to think about. Those thoughts of the unpleasant imagined outcome, something that has not happened yet, cause you to be uncomfortable. Replace those thoughts with pleasant ones... Think about your dreams, your ambitions, and achieving your goals. Think about how satisfying it will be to hear a customer say, "Yes, I'll buy that." Think about how nice it will be to hear your boss say, "Great work!" Focus your thoughts on a pleasant outcome. That turns fear off and allows you to get back to selling. Then, take action! Do something positive right away. Make a call. Go see a customer. Do a report. Begin working at whatever you put off doing. When you make progress on it, even a little, you can congratulate yourself on your bravery! Yes, bravery. You are also exhibiting self-control and discipline—attributes people in all cultures of the world respect and admire.

With your fear and stress significantly reduced, the sales job becomes fun. Successful salespeople love to go to work because they can enjoy their jobs with hardly any stress. The sales goal is always there of course. The work, however, is always easier when you have the right tools (like the *ABC's of Selling with Etiquette*)!

Turn the page to learn another essential concept of selling.

Fear melts when you take action towards a goal you really want.

*– Robert G Allen, real estate multi-millionaire
and best-selling author*

 is for Goal

To get there, you need to know where you are going.

An old saying states that a journey of a thousand miles begins with the first step. That same journey, if the proper goal is set before you start, may take only 500 miles! A goal is, in its simplest form, deciding precisely where you want to go. People moving toward a goal achieve more faster than people who are just wandering.

The first thing you do every morning is set a goal. When you first wake up, you set a goal for what you are going to do next. You may decide to hit "snooze" and get 10 minutes of sleep. You may decide to hop out of bed and head for the coffee pot. Either way, you decide, then you move. That is the simplest example of goal setting. You use the same process to make yourself successful at selling. You decide what to do, then you set a goal to do it. Goals work by focusing your actions.

"I'm going to do ____," is a basic goal. People instinctively think in the form of goals. We decide what we are going to do. That is the primary goal. Then we plan the steps we must take to get that job done. Those are intermediate goals.

How do you accomplish a huge goal? Chop your big goals into little goals. Set little goals for yourself that, when you accomplish them, will add up to success! How do you eat an elephant? One bite at a time!

You probably will not know how to accomplish every goal. No problem. Ask someone who has already done it. Read books on the subject. Learn how they did it before. Then, analyze your situation. Perhaps you can invent a new way to get the large goal accomplished. Perhaps not. What matters most is learning how the system works; then you can set your smaller goals and begin working to achieve them.

Setting goals is an effective way to get things done in the shortest possible time. Time, after all, is our most valuable asset. The more we can accomplish in the time we have, the better-off we are. Goals are very effective time management tools.

Another effective tool is a butter knife. It is a great tool for spreading jelly on bread, but it would be lousy for cutting down a tree. For cutting down trees, you need a powerful chainsaw. To accomplish big things in sales, you need goals that are more like chainsaws than butter knives. For goals that are as powerful as chainsaws, apply the M.A.C. principle.

M.A.C. stands for Measurable, Achievable and Challenging. M.A.C. goals provide more focus and faster results. Here is how they work...

Measurable goals must include some action that anyone can easily measure. "I am going to sell 15 magazines today" is a measurable goal. It tells everyone who is going to sell (I am), how many I will sell (15), what will be sold (magazines) and when they will be sold (today). "I am going to sell something" is much less measurable and much less effective. Measurable goals allow you to keep track of exactly how well you are doing and keep you focused on reaching your exact goal. Measurability keeps your goals sharp like a chainsaw's cutting chain.

Achievable goals keep us from becoming discouraged and quitting. If you set an impossible goal, you will fail. Nobody likes to fail. Why waste your time trying to reach an impossible goal? Make sure all your goals are achievable so that you can go to work every day with a good chance of success. Achievability keeps us as tough and on-the-job as a chainsaw.

Challenging goals keep us working harder. When you set challenging goals, you set yourself up to outperform yourself (and others). To set challenging goals, decide how much you can do and then add a little more to it. Challenging goals will drive you to sell more and to make more money. Challenging puts power in our goals like the gas puts power in the chainsaw. Be careful! Gasoline is dangerous, and so are challenging goals. Always balance your goals to make them achievable, as well as challenging. Then you will find yourself routinely surprising others with how much you can accomplish.

This basic concept, a measurable, achievable and challenging goal, may be one of the most important. With great goals, you can do great things!

Nothing is particularly hard, as long as you divide it into small jobs.

– Henry Ford, Founder of Ford Motor Company

Etiquette Essentials
Gossip

Gossip is the sharing of unpleasant information about other people. Whether the information is true or false does not matter, gossiping is harmful. Gossip hurts the person you are talking about, and it hurts you! How? People who enjoy spreading rumors are like sharks. They spend their time hunting and attacking weaker fish. But what happens as soon as one of their own gets injured? The rest turn on the injured one and rip it to shreds!

In sales, you spend your time talking to many people. All of those people have networks with other people. Gossip spreads. You cannot control where it goes. It would be easy for you to lose a sale because a customer has learned about something negative you said previously. Spend your time sharing positive information. People will associate you with good news. You will gain a reputation for being a positive person and you will never lose a sale because of gossip.

Be positive about your competition too. If a customer talks about a competitive product, avoid saying negative things about it. Just listen, and then turn the conversation back onto your product. Spreading bad information about a competitive product can hurt you. Customers want you to talk about your products, not bash the competition. Besides, whenever you and your customer are talking about a competitive product, you are not talking about the benefits of yours! You will sell more by promoting the benefits of your product rather than by gossiping about the competition!

 # is for Honesty

How you can work less and earn more!

Honesty is telling the truth in everything you say. When you consistently tell the truth, people learn to trust you. Customers are always looking for an honest salesperson. Over time, honesty builds trust. Trust builds positive RELATIONSHIPS. Positive relationships bring your customer back to you to buy more. Honesty usually pays off in repeat business.

Honest salespeople sell more and work less. When you only tell the truth, you only have to remember one story, one set of facts. People who lie are constantly working harder. They must work to remember what story they told to this person and what other story they told to a different person. People who lie are always under stress. They are always worried about someone catching them in their untruths. Who needs that kind of stress on top of the normal workday stress we all feel? After a while, dishonest people must work extra hard to cover their lies as the truth comes out.

By the way, the truth always comes out. It may be weeks or years later, but the truth eventually surfaces. If you lie and you are caught, that destroys any trust and any relationship you established with your customers. You may lose their business and may not get it back. Your reputation is tarnished.

Honesty is easier. When you always tell the truth, you avoid the stress of deceiving people. What happens if you must deliver bad news to your customers? That causes stress. It certainly does, but the stress of giving customers bad news lasts only a while, then it is over. If, for example, a customer's order will arrive late, it is much better to let them know as soon as possible. They will be disappointed and they may be angry. It would be much worse however to wait and let the customer discover the problem as it happens. Telling them the truth early allows them to adjust their plans and work around the problem. Giving customers bad news early shows them that you are more concerned about their order and their business then you are about yourself. It can actually help customers trust you more.

Selling is all about working with people. Since that is true, is it okay to tell just a little lie to keep from hurting someone's feelings? No. Saying nothing is better than lying, and telling the truth may even help that person in the end.

Everyone knows the story of the wife who asks her husband, "Does this dress make me look fat?" (In this case, yes, it does. Trust me. It really does!) If the husband lies and says no, her friends (or worse, a perfect stranger) will say something later that lets her know exactly how fat she looks in that dress. She has her feelings crushed, and it did not have to happen.

Be honest, but not rash or foolish… Just because you discover a problem or an unpleasant fact does not mean you have to broadcast it to the world. Yes, you should always be honest. You should be tactful at the same time. In the example above, the husband could tactfully say, "That dress doesn't make you look nearly as beautiful as you really are. Why don't you wear another one?" Not being stupid, the husband knows there is no reason to insult his wife. He also prevented her from being embarrassed later. Notice that he did not ignore the problem. Avoiding an answer would have resulted in a bad situation too. He truthfully and tactfully addressed the situation and offered a solution.

Honesty is a key habit of successful selling. Never think that being dishonest or avoiding a customer problem will make your life easier. It will not. Be honest with good news and bad. You will build a trusting relationship between you and all your customers. You will sell more, and enjoy a life with less stress.

Honesty is the cornerstone of all success, without which confidence and ability to perform shall cease to exist.

– Mary Kay Ash, Founder of Mary Kay Cosmetics

Etiquette Essentials
A Few Good Habits

Along with the good habit of telling the truth, there are a few habits of etiquette that help build trust and earn respect from others…

Many people wear hats in the winter. Caps are especially popular these days, and some company uniforms include hats. Hat etiquette is simple. Take them off when you go inside. If there is no place to hang your hat, carry it around with you.

The same applies to sunglasses. Take them off when you go inside. Customers will be uncomfortable talking to you if they cannot see your eyes. This applies also if you are having a conversation outside. If you are selling outside, take your sunglasses off. Let your customer see your eyes! They will automatically have more trust in what you are saying.

Handshakes are very important. They "tell" another person a lot about you in a very small amount of time. Shake hands confidently! That is not the same as bone-crushingly hard! Simply grasp the other person's hand lightly, and apply enough pressure to be felt. Hold it for about the time it takes to say, "Hello," then let go.

Avoid these two handshakes that harm your image: The "dead fish" handshake, one with no pressure at all, tells the other person, "I really do not care about you." A "bone-crusher" handshake tells the other person, "Watch out for me, I will try to dominate this meeting." Both of those handshakes give the other person a bad impression of you.

Pay attention to the person whose hand you are shaking. (Note: Only desperate politicians and con men actually shake someone's hand up and down before they let go.) People who earn their living with their hands (surgeons, musicians, etc.) will shake hands lightly or avoid shaking hands with you. That is perfectly fine. If you allow the other person to make the first move for a handshake, then you will never be left standing embarrassed with your hand out in front of you.

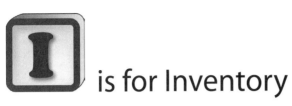 is for Inventory

Everything you have to sell is in your mind.

INVENTORY is the word that describes the group of products (or services) a salesperson has to sell. If you are a salesperson in a shoe store, your inventory is all the sizes and styles of shoes in the store. It is also all the shoelaces, socks, shoe polish and accessories. If you are an insurance salesperson, your inventory is all of the different insurance policies your company offers. If you are a politician running for office, your inventory is all your qualifications, experiences and personality strengths.

Salespeople must be very familiar with their inventory. It does not matter if a company has 200 different products to sell. If the salespeople only know about two of them, only those two products will sell. Salespeople must study the inventory. They must acquire this knowledge to be effective in selling all the products.

The more you know about your products, the easier it is for you to sell them. You can quickly decide which product will best match what your customers want. You must know all the important facts and benefits of your products. Then you can present them in a convincing, enthusiastic way so your customers can easily see the value in your products. When they see that value, customers are more likely to buy from you.

Did you know that you can only focus your attention on one thing at a time? You can consider many things in quick succession, but you can only really concentrate on one thing at a time. In selling, always focus your attention on what your customer is saying. If you have to concentrate on remembering things about your inventory (what products do or how much they cost), you will miss something important your customer tells you. Learning your inventory in advance avoids that.

You should know these facts about any product in your inventory:

- **Who** can use it?
- **What** is it used for? What sizes, colors, etc. are available?
- **When** should it be used?
- **Where** should it be used?
- **How** should it be used, and how much does it cost?
- **Why** customers would buy it, not a competitive product?

Restaurant waiters who know their menu make better recommendations and much bigger tips! Store clerks sell more (and earn more commissions) if they lead customers quickly to products in their stores. As you can see, it really pays to know your inventory well!

The future you see is the future you get.

*– Robert G. Allen, real estate multi-millionaire
and best-selling author*

Etiquette Essentials
Introductions

In business, it is not who you know but who knows you that makes you successful. An introduction is the most effective way to meet people. You can provide a valuable service to your customers and friends by introducing them to the other people you know.

The first step is to know the names of both people. You need to know both people before you can introduce them to each other. Introduce the most notable person last. ("Save the best for last," is how you remember that.)

Here is an example of a standard introduction: You are at a business function with your boss, Sarah Brasher, and a salesperson you know from another company approaches. You make the introduction this way... "Sarah Brasher, this is Mike Walker a salesperson with Hardy and Associates. Mike Walker, this is Sarah Brasher, my Director of Sales."

That is all there is to an introduction. You said each person's name and the job they do. They can exchange business cards and take the conversation further if they want to talk more. It is up to them. They will both be grateful to you because they will not have to stand there wondering who the other person is.

A Different Perspective: Be a Better Buyer!

When you are the customer, you can use your understanding of the twenty-six selling basics in this book to make better purchases. As a buyer, you can understand and predict what salespeople will do. As a buyer, you can grade your salespeople to separate the selling professionals from the amateurs. Everyone would rather work with a professional salesperson who will deliver the service you like and cares more about what you want than what he wants to sell. As a buyer who understands the essential concepts of selling, you can immediately recognize the best value; and you can tell when the price is right for you. You will never have to suffer through dealings with amateur salespeople again. Now, you can spot them in a minute, and quietly move on to work with a "pro" to get the kind of service you give your customers!

Save yourself some valuable time and do not try to teach these selling basics to salespeople who are trying to sell you something. If they are great salespeople, they already use these basics. If they are not so great, they probably will not be interested in your critique of their efforts (or lack of effort). If you do run across a bright person whom you think would really sell better if only they understood the essential concepts of selling, then please recommend this book to them.

Your recommendation will produce at least three benefits:

1) An up-and-coming salesperson who learns to use the essential concepts of selling will sell more. He will begin to enjoy his work because understanding the basics helps him achieve sales goals and make more money!

2) Their customers will benefit. The essential concepts of selling shift the focus of salespeople from themselves to their customers. Customers are much more comfortable and satisfied with confident salespeople who are great at all concepts of selling.

3) You will benefit from feeling good about helping someone improve their life. You know the old saying, "Give a man a fish and he can eat for a day. Teach him to fish and he can eat for a lifetime." Selling is like fishing!

Your recommendation creates a win, win, win, situation! Hold on! Another essential selling concept awaits you…

 is for Join

Step into your customer's world.
That's where the money is!

We each live in our own little world. Salespeople who join their customer's world sell more (and earn more) than self-centered or aloof salespeople. Whenever you are around other people, you have two options: You can focus inward, or you can reach outward. In selling, you can focus your attention on yourself, or you can concentrate on your customers, the ones who can buy your products.

Your customers live in their own unique, problem-filled worlds. They are always concerned about getting what they want. They are not concerned about you. They are not concerned about what you are selling. Always keep this in mind when you are working with customers. From a customer viewpoint, the most important thing about your product is: It is not important. What is important is what the customer wants.

Your job as a salesperson is to reach out and join your customers in their current world. The fastest way to do that is to ask customers questions. With questions, you can discover what they want.

You need to be careful and sincere when you ask customers these questions. Trust this: Trust this: Most customers are not spending their day trying to find salespeople to invite into their world! They are trying to find whatever it is that they want. You need to be careful and sincere when you ask customers these questions. Customers will quickly put up a wall to avoid insincere salespeople who act friendly just to make a sale. You can climb over that wall using the ladder called "sincerity." Be sincere as you focus on your customer and the problem they wish to solve (or the product they wish to buy). You can bring your customer good value, and you will be providing the service the customer is seeking. For that, your customer will let you join a part of their world. Here

DALE BRAKHAGE & EDIE HAND

are some good examples of questions that will let you join your customer's world when you talk about products:

- What do you have in mind?
- What do you want this product to do for you?
- Are there any special things you are looking for?

You can also make customers feel more comfortable with you by finding common interests. As you work with the same customers repeatedly, you can build lasting relationships by taking care of their business first, then discovering what else you have in common. It may be a hobby like cars, music or animals. It may be an interest in the same sports team, or you may have mutual friends. As you join their world, you build a valuable relationship with that customer. As you help customers repeatedly, over time they will invite you into more of their world. You eventually become friends. That happens when they decide it should.

If you have ever joined a sports team or the military, you remember that you had to put on their uniform to join. They did not change their uniforms to match the way you looked, did they? Do not expect customers to change in order to join your world.

People like to do business with their friends. Use questions to find out what your customers want so that they will buy from you today. Use empathy to build relationships so that your customer will buy from you tomorrow. Empathy is putting yourself in your customer's place, thinking as they think and wanting what they want. Empathy allows you to get close to your customers. Empathy allows you to join their world. Salespeople with empathy let what the customer wants guide their actions.

The first step toward selling with empathy is to pay attention to your customer. Look carefully to determine the customer's mood by watching how they walk, talk, etc. If the customer is happy, you can act happy too. If, however, the customer is obviously having a bad day, the last thing in the world they want is an overly cheery salesperson. Follow the customer's lead to make a positive connection. The connections you make after the first impression are the basis for building a positive relationship. By making positive connections, you will build positive relationships and make friends who will want to buy from you repeatedly. If you make negative impressions, the customer will push you away and you will not make a sale.

51

How do you make a good connection? Find out what the customer likes. This is easy for outside sales people. They go into customers' offices. Customers' offices are full of clues about what they like. Family photos, diplomas, hobby photos, sports team souvenirs, etc., all show what the customer likes. The best salespeople notice those clues and bring them up in conversation. This shows the customer that the salesperson is interested in them, not just in a sale.

Inside salespeople have fewer clues and often see customers only once. Store clerks and restaurant servers know that it is almost impossible to establish a friendship in one visit. You can, however, make a good first impression and leave a lasting positive impression. Customers will remember you and come back to see you again.

Etiquette Essentials
Jokes

Jokes are funny stories, and everybody enjoys a good joke occasionally. When you are in a selling situation, be very careful telling jokes. Your customer may not have the same sense of humor you have. If you tell a joke and your customer does not think it is funny, then you have wasted valuable time.

Time spent actually selling to a customer is very important. Most customers cannot spend hours chatting with you, so wasting their time telling jokes is dangerous. Even if the customer thinks your joke is funny, you have still used valuable time.

Sending jokes via e-mail is an even worse waste of time. Save your e-mails for serious business. Customers receive so much spam e-mail already. You do not want your busy customers to delete your e-mails before they read them because they think it is another joke.

When you take the time to join your customer's world, you will discover if they enjoy jokes or not. The safest, best way to enjoy jokes with a customer is to let the customer tell them.

Learn to create your life from the inside out. When you reach out to ask your customer personal things that matter to him you are no longer on the sideline. Caring comes across as REAL.

– Edie Hand

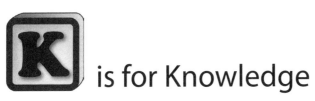 is for Knowledge

More valuable than gold, and free for the taking!

Knowledge is critical to successful selling. Salespeople who know more about their inventory, customers, TERRITORY, price and competition will sell more than salespeople who know less. There are two reasons for this... First, knowledge gives a salesperson confidence! Second, customers are more comfortable buying from a confident salesperson.

There is good news and bad news about knowledge. Here is the bad news: The only way you acquire knowledge is by studying. You can learn by watching others, by listening or by reading, but you must actively participate. You have to work at learning. You must spend some of your valuable time to learn something.

Now for the good news! There are two bits of good news: First, as you work at learning, you get better at it. As you discover the most effective ways for your brain to learn information, you literally learn how you learn. The more you study, the easier studying becomes for you. Second, gaining knowledge is up to you alone. You decide when, where, and how much you want to learn. You are in charge, and you do not have to wait on anyone's approval to gain knowledge! The knowledge you want is out there and you can have as much as you want.

Another way to think about knowledge truly demonstrates its value: Knowledge is worth what it costs you plus whatever you gain from it. What does knowledge cost you? It costs you your time obviously. When you spend an hour of your life learning, you can never get that hour back. The richest nation in the world cannot buy back one hour that already passed. Your time is incredibly valuable!

The value of knowledge includes what you can gain from it. You could spend your valuable time goofing off or doing destructive things. You would gain nothing from those activities. Yet with knowledge, you can create art, build a new business, build a new friendship, sell effectively, etc. When knowledge is applied effectively with dedication, you can change your life for the better and you can improve the lives of those around you. Second only to time, knowledge is your most valuable asset.

Unlike irreplaceable time however, you can have as much knowledge as you desire! In addition, knowledge stays with you. Unlike money, gold or gasoline, which are gone as soon as you use them, your knowledge increases as you use it! With knowledge, you are free to change the world around you. Without knowledge, the world will freely change you.

Risk comes from not knowing what you're doing.

– Warren Buffett multi-billionaire investor

Etiquette Essentials
Hugs and Kisses

Kissing hands of the ladies or kissing a man on the cheek were once acceptable greetings. That is no longer the case. Kissing has almost disappeared in business situations in America. Leave kissing for social situations.

Hugging, however, has recently made a comeback. Business people who know each other and like each other might share a business-like hug when they meet. The proper way to give a business associate a hug is from the side. As you move up towards the person, stand beside them, place your hand around their shoulder, and give a slight hug. Hugging hard and hugging face-to-face are both too intimate for use in business situations. The safe way to use hugging is to let other people hug you first. That way you will never be embarrassed trying to hug someone who is NOT interested in that sort of thing.

A Different Perspective: Where is all the knowledge?

Selling is a complete mystery to most people. If most high schools and universities taught selling instead of Algebra 2, there would be many more efficient salespeople and buyers! (Everyone who hated Algebra 2 say, "Yeah!")

Why do schools very rarely teach selling? Why does the business of buying and selling stumble along inefficiently? The answer to those questions is the fact that effective selling is too valuable to give away! Big companies train their salespeople to sell effectively. They spend enormous sums to make their salespeople better than the competition. The return on that investment is more sales and more market share. Do you think those major corporations will sponsor classes in schools to prepare better salespeople for other companies? No.

Most small and medium sized businesses do not have the resources to train salespeople well. Those companies make up most of our economy. So, most salespeople learn their selling skills through on-the-job-training (OJT). In other words, they learn as they go. They try, fail and learn from their mistakes. If they cannot learn fast enough, they leave.

Occasionally, individuals figure it out. Somehow, they start applying sales basics. They sell more and earn more for their success. They enjoy the thrill that comes from successful sales. They earn recognition and awards. Many become wealthy through sales. Only a few of these successful salespeople become sales trainers and pass along their knowledge to others. Most successful salespeople keep their knowledge to themselves. Their "how to sell" knowledge gives them a great lifestyle and a lot of money. Why give those valuable secrets away, especially to someone who may compete with them later for a sale?

Something is wrong with a system that lets a few successful people and companies hoard powerful knowledge like this. Everyone should be able to learn how to be more persuasive and sell more. The fact that you are reading this book demonstrates that you agree that this knowledge is valuable enough to share. Please pass it along to other people you know. Recommend this book to others. No one should ever have to be uncomfortable persuading others in the value of a good idea. Education can make all of us more persuasive! So, back to the education...

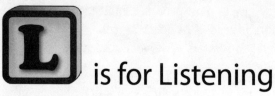 # is for Listening

To sell more, talk less!

Nothing you can tell a customer will let you know what they are willing to buy. Everything a customer tells you can help you sell.

Customers know what they want to buy, and they will tell you. You have to listen. Amazingly, either most salespeople do not know how to listen, or they do not care to listen to customers. Why? It is much easier to recite a memorized sales speech than it is to engage the customer in an actual sales conversation. Another reason is most salespeople are more concerned about themselves and their product than they are concerned about their customers. Salespeople who love to give fact-filled speeches to customers sell less than salespeople who really listen to discover their customers' wants.

The best salespeople do not give sales speeches. They have conversations with customers. They ask questions. They listen intently to their customers' answers. After the customers describe what they want to buy, the salespeople then describe benefits that the customers will receive from their purchases. Benefits sell.

The good news about listening is that anyone who can hear can learn to listen effectively. There is a foolproof system of listening. It is a system, not just a skill, because listening is a set of complex behaviors. Effective listening is much more than not talking.

Have you ever heard of active listening? Active listening is a tool taught in schools and businesses to improve communications. Active listening involves looking at the speaker, not interrupting, focusing your thoughts on what the speaker is saying instead of what you are going to say next, and giving positive feedback signals to let the speaker know you are listening. Good salespeople use active listening. It is a very effective tool. However, there is more to effective listening. The best salespeople take active listening

DALE BRAKHAGE & EDIE HAND

even further. They use the three-steps of a more effective listening process: Complete Listening.

Step One: **Proactive** Listening
Step Two: **Interactive** Listening
Step Three: **Reactive** Listening

The first step in Complete Listening is **Proactive Listening**. Proactive Listening is *preparing to listen*. Drop what you are doing, clear your mind of everything else and focus your attention on what the customer is going to say next. Turn your body towards the customer and look completely focused on them. (You would not throw a ball to someone who was not looking at you, ready to catch it. Why would someone throw information to you if you were not looking at him or her, ready to hear it?)

The second step of Complete Listening is **Interactive Listening**. Interactive Listening is *receiving the information*. It is truly active listening. Focus your thoughts on receiving their information. Look at the speaker. Lean in slightly and nod occasionally to show your interest. Give occasional positive feedback to show the speaker you are receiving their message. Take notes, if it is appropriate. Ask questions to clarify your understanding, but only if you really need to ask. Do not ask questions to take over the conversation. With Interactive Listening, you really focus on learning what the other people have to say. They will tell you exactly what they want to buy.

The third step in Complete Listening is **Reactive Listening**. Reactive listening is *analyzing and processing the important information* the customer just gave you. Is it important? Yes! All information from customers is important. Some information is more important because it helps you sell your product right now, but all of it is important. Customers may tell you something you can use later, so keep good records. Take notes, and file the information you decide is most important. As soon as you can, plan your next step to sell that customer something else. Based upon what you have learned, decide what your next sales action should be. Plan when you should do it, and enter the actions on your calendar.

Reactive Listening is new to most salespeople. It is the step between customer contact and your follow-up. Inside salespeople can use Reactive

Listening every day. It happens in a few seconds, during your conversation with a walk-in customer. The customer gives you information, and you have a few seconds to evaluate the customer's wants and then show the customer your product that best suits them.

Reactive Listening could also take hours following a first outside sales visit on a potential new corporate customer. Large corporate deals may take weeks or months to win, so you do not want to lose any time by not capturing the important information the customer gave you. The fastest way to make a sale is to react the right way to all the information that a customer provides.

One of the fastest ways to lose a sale is to lose information. Customers remember what they tell you. If you do not care enough about them to listen and to remember what they said, why should they buy from you?

A special listening challenge is the angry customer. Everyone eventually has an out-of-control angry customer. Think of that customer as a hurricane. They are going to blow, and nothing you can do can stop them. So do not try. A hurricane can blow over the strongest tree, and an angry customer can blow over any strong-willed salesperson. The key to surviving the onslaught is flexibility. Bend in the wind! Let them vent. Right or wrong, they feel so strongly in that moment that they simply must vent their feelings. It is just too bad that you are the nearest salesperson at the time!

In this situation, remain in a neutral non-combative attitude. Listen attentively without smiling or frowning. Take an interest in their position, but do not take a hard position of your own, either for or against them. After they have "blown off some steam" and they seem ready for a two-way conversation, tell them you understand how they might feel that way. (That is not the same thing as telling them they are right.)

If you have listened well, you will know what the customer wants. If it is justified and if it is in your power to grant that, then go ahead. If it is not in your power, then your best move is to seek help from your manager. If you are your own manager, it is still a good idea to tell the customer you will get back to them after you have investigated the matter. Most of the time, you do not have to make an on-the-spot decision. If you are human, listening to an angry customer makes you a little upset. That is okay and normal. You will make a better decision after you have had time to cool down and think about what is best for your business.

The old adage, "The customer is always right," really means, "The customer always wins a fight." It never pays to fight with an angry customer. You both lose, and the customer might spend years creating and spreading wild stories about your company's horrible service.

Etiquette Essentials
Be on Time

Do NOT be LATE. That is that; period, the end.

If you come late to an appointment or meeting, it means you do not care. The other people at the meeting will see you as unprofessional. It will be up to you to spend your valuable time to try to regain their trust and respect. That is why you should never be late to any business function. Of course, things happen, and you may find yourself running late. Call ahead. Let them know that you will be late and where you are. Make that call before your meeting is to start. If you do that, the others at the meeting can use their time wisely. They might decide to wait for you, or they might decide to do something else. Either way, they will appreciate you for respecting their valuable time.

Just being at work on time, every day sends a message to your company that you are serious about your job. Being late to work sends a message too: You are not that serious. Who do you think bosses like best? On-time employees or late ones?

A Different Perspective: Train your brain!

You trust yourself more than you trust any other person. If you tell yourself something, you tend to believe it. If you tell yourself something enough times, you will believe it. This is a form of self-hypnosis, and it can be a very powerful force in your life. In college as I studied psychology, we experimented with a particular type of mental programming. The purpose of the experiment was to "train our brains," to program them to do something subconsciously without our consciously thinking about it. The subconscious portion of your brain is always working. It controls your body's physiological functions, it coordinates your movements, it records every detail of every day, it dreams when you are asleep, etc. It is vastly more powerful than the conscious portion of the brain with which you actively think when you are awake and concentrating.

To program our subconscious brain to work for us, we wrote down short rhymes that contained a positive idea and an action phrase. The positive idea was "bait" to make the rhyme appealing to our subconscious. The action phrase contained a measurable activity. It contained these elements: Who, what, and where. It was something we would consciously recognize when it worked.

My programming rhyme was, "I'm the luckiest guy I know, I find money everywhere I go, just lying around in the street." I wrote that idea down and read it aloud dozens of time a day for several weeks. Can you guess what happened? I began to find money: pennies, nickels, dimes, quarters, even dollar bills! Other people walked right over them, but my subconscious brain spotted them for me. Thirty years later, I still reinforce that idea, and I still find money in the street almost every day. It is a lot of fun, and profitable!

There has been much scientific work on the subject of subconscious mental programming. If you are interested, and will spend the time, you can train your brain to think positively, to lose weight, to stop smoking, to be on time, etc. If you are interested in this topic, search the internet for self-hypnosis. That search will provide you with a large source of books and sites to investigate.

Learn to read non-verbal communication because it tells a real story.

– Edie Hand

 is for More

Everybody wants more, and YOU can give it to them!

Everybody wants more. We all want to feel like we got the better part of any deal. We always want to get the best value for the price we had to pay. Customers who believe they received more when they purchased from someone usually do two things:

They brag to their friends about their deal.

They come back to buy again.

Many restaurants in the United States understand this "more" concept very well. They serve you more food than you can possibly eat. The servers keep refilling your drink glass too. This "extra" service does not cost the restaurant very much, but it makes a big impression on the customers. Those customers usually brag to their friends about the great deal they got, and they come back to that restaurant to eat again!

Many clothing stores offer free alterations for one year on any clothes you buy. Most people do not change size much, and most people who do will not bother getting clothes altered. Those stores make customers happy by offering more, the free alteration service. In this case, it is free to the store as well, if nobody uses it. Another example of this is a free towing service if your new car breaks down. Since most new cars do not break down, this service costs the car dealer very little. The lesson here is this: You do not have to give anything away to satisfy the customer's desire for more.

Whatever you are selling, find a way to give your customer more. Even if it is just a tiny thing, your customer will appreciate getting more. For example, after you sell a shirt, show the customer the spare button that is sewn onto the hem. After you sell someone a hamburger and fries, drop a few extra fries into their to-go bag. After you sell a car, tell the customer they can bring it back for a free car wash. All of these examples will pay for themselves by the free word-of-mouth advertising you receive as your customers happily brag to their friends about the good deal they made. You give them a chance to look smart to their peers for their shrewd shopping. Besides that, they will be much more likely to come back and buy from you again.

A simple way to give your customer more is to always promise less and deliver more. Whenever you can, promise your customer a service that you know you can improve upon. For example, promise your customer delivery that is later than you know you can provide. Most customers will be happy when you can deliver their product "early."

Caution: Always, always, promise less and deliver more, not the other way around! If you promise more but deliver less, be ready for your customer to have a wonderful time telling horror stories about your poor service to anyone who will listen to them. People like to tell others about a good deal they made, but they love to tell horror stories about poor service. People are like that.

This basic concept teaches us that effort affects sales. The more effort you put into your selling, the more sales you will make. It takes additional effort on your part to think of ways to give your customers greater service. It would take less work to coast along, selling like everyone else. That little extra effort however can come back to you in many additional sales. Put sticky notes with the word "MORE" on the dashboard of your car and on your bathroom mirror to remind you to start doing more (and selling more)! It takes 21 days to form a new habit, so in just three weeks, you can form the habit of doing more for your customers. Try this concept soon. You will see results right away.

Tell three people today you care about them and their success. Watch for real rewards.

– Edie Hand

Etiquette Essentials
Table Manners

Using good table manners makes a positive impression on customers when you share a meal with them. The opposite is also true. Poor manners make long-lasting negative impressions on customers. Using good table manners always makes sense when you are dining out. You never know who could be watching you from across the room. It is a good idea for you to learn good table manners. Study articles or books on the subject. Become an expert in table manners, and people will enjoy dining with you.

Here are some basic points of etiquette for meals. First, some "do's." Place your napkin in your lap when you first sit down. Watch what your host orders, and order items that cost similarly. Wait until everyone at the table has food before you begin eating. Taste your food before adding salt, pepper or condiments. Eat slowly and carefully, and please chew with your mouth closed. Be certain to thank your host for the meal when it is over.

Now, here are some "do not's." Do not slurp your drinks. Do not speed-eat, holding the next bite of food in the air in front of you before you have finished swallowing the first one. Do not talk with your mouth full. Do not wipe your plate with bread to pick up the last bits of food. Do not spill your food on yourself or anyone else! Do not eat food off anyone else's plate! Do not steal tips off other tables! Okay, okay. These "do not's" progressed into the ridiculous. The main point of meal etiquette to remember is this: Be on your best behavior whenever you share a meal. Customers will not do business with you just because you have excellent table manners. There are many stories however of customers who would not do business with a salesperson who displayed poor table manners at a meal. Now that is some food for thought.

 is for No

No means "Ask me why."

"No" is the most important word in selling. Without the word no, there is no need for salespeople! Businesses would only need order-takers to service all the customers lined up waiting to buy. Be thankful for the word no.

Salespeople understand that all selling begins with the customer thinking no. No is a person's natural state of mind. No protects us from buying things we do not need and from doing things we do not want to do. No puts us in charge. A two-year old can take charge of two adult parents by simply saying "No!" and refusing to eat. After a while, the parents will do anything to get the child to eat.

When your customer says no, they think, "I do not believe the value of your product is worth the price." It is nothing personal. Customers will naturally think no until they believe the product has enough value to make them want it. Then they buy.

You persuade customers to say yes by explaining enough benefits so the customer believes the product has value. Every sale follows the same format. Customers begin the buying process saying no to every product. As they begin to realize that they have a problem to solve, they begin to want some item. When they really want to solve that problem or obtain that item, they start to shop around until they see a product that attracts them with the benefits it offers. They compare items, and when they discover a product that has more than enough benefits to outweigh the price, they buy it. The more benefits a product offers the more value the customer sees in it. Until they believe the value of the product is worth the price, customers will say no to buying anything.

There are hundreds of ways for customers to say no. Some of them are:

• Not today.

- Maybe later.
- It is not my size.
- It costs too much.
- I do not have time.
- It is the wrong color.
- It makes me look fat.
- Let me think about it.
- Call me back tomorrow.
- My wife will not like it.
- This is not a good time.
- Yes, okay. (What a liar!)
- I am going to shop around first.
- Can you give me a better deal?
- (And the particularly effective...) "That sounds good. Why don't you check back with me in a few weeks?"

There are just as many reasons why a customer may say no. Customers say no if your product is not useful to them. Either they do not have a problem your product can solve, or they do not believe your product is able to solve a problem they have. In order to persuade them to say yes, you need to discover the exact reason they are not buying. Once you know that reason, you can address it specifically. It is your right and your responsibility to ask a customer why they say no.

Just as polite people naturally say, "Bless you," after someone sneezes, salespeople should naturally ask "Why?" after a customer says no. I recommend that you do not loudly blurt out, "Why?" That word, used alone, can come across as pushy or aggressive. It is much more effective to use a softer, conversational tone. Your goal is to keep the conversation going in order to discover the real reason behind the no.

Here are many non-threatening, easy ways to ask why. Make sure you smile as you ask your brief question.

"May I please ask why?"
"Oh? What makes you say that?"
"Will you please share your reason for that?"
"Is there a particular reason why?"

"Why you would say that?

The point of all these questions is to learn the customer's real reason for not buying. When the customer shares the reason for not buying, then it is your turn to talk. Never argue. To make the sale, you have to help the customer see enough value in what you are selling so that they want to buy it. You can read how to do that in the chapters on Value and Want.

Etiquette Essentials
Keep Your Cool

Be cool when you hear "No" from customers, or when you say no to others. By cool, I mean considerate. Respect the other person's opinion, and remember, it is just business. In business, you leave your personal feelings out of it. We all get frustrated from rejection, but never, never take out your frustrations on someone else. Be especially careful to treat other salespeople considerately. Those people trying to sell you something deserve your respect, even as you tell them, "No, thank you." Put yourself in their shoes for a moment, and join their world. Treat them with the same respect and dignity you would like to hear from your customers when they must tell you no.

A Different Perspective: Plastic combs, drugs and keys.

I stunk on my first job as a salesperson. When my high school band director asked us to sell packages of plastic combs for a fundraiser, I froze. Other band kids had no problem going door-to-door selling those combs. Not me, I avoided it as long as I could and sold only a few—just enough to get by. The problem was that I thought about it too much. I did not know how to sell, so I avoided it. That was strange because I was a persuasive person. I had no problem "selling" my ideas to my family and friends. I did not know what to say to customers, and I was afraid that people would say no. (Of course they would! Everyone thinks and says no until you show them the benefits of what you are selling.) If I knew then how selling worked, I would have been okay with that and I would have sold a hundred of those plastic combs!

Years later, after college and time in the Army, I applied for sales jobs. Research told me the fastest way into corporate management was through sales. A large pharmaceutical firm hired me because I had enthusiasm, military self-discipline and extensive chemical weapons knowledge. To them, that meant I understood biochemistry and they could trust me to work on my own.

For five 14-hour days, my manager and a trainer tag-team trained me. They explained precisely how the job worked: who to see, what to say, where to go, and when to see the doctors. At night, I studied our drugs and the competition. I memorized the information and passed all their tests. I asked tons of "what-if" questions, and they answered them all.

On the afternoon of the last day of training, I was ready to start my new sales career. The manager told me to drive him to the airport and to stop along the way to make my very first sales call. I was confident and so serious (and yet just a little nervous) as I parked the car at the doctor's office. The manager went in with me, and the sales call went just as we had trained! I presented the products, and the doctor said he would definitely use them for his patients! My manager just smiled the whole time.

I felt wonderful! As we left the office, my manager asked a question I still remember whenever I am making sales calls. "Dale, how are you planning to get your keys out of the car?" I had locked my keys in the car! My manager had seen me do it, and that is why he had been smiling! He thought it was hilarious! Anyway, I sheepishly got the car unlocked and drove him to the airport in time for his flight.

What a difference between the high school kid who would not sell plastic combs and the professional pharmaceutical salesperson! My new understanding of sales made the very positive difference. I hope that this book will help you understand sales so you can enjoy selling too. Perhaps it will even save you from locking your keys in the car! Now it is time to learn another valuable essential concept...

Succeeding is not really a life experience that does that much good. Failing is a much more sobering and enlightening experience.

– Michael Eisner, CEO of the Walt Disney Company

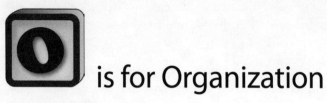 **is for Organization**

Teamwork for one!

Everyone knows the value of teamwork. Teamwork focuses the efforts of a group into a single powerful force. What teamwork does for a group, ORGANIZATION does for an individual. Organization focuses the efforts of any individual into a single powerful force.

Organization allows you to accomplish more in your day. The number one trait of award-winning salespeople is not a pleasant personality. It is not a pretty face. It is not good communication skills. In over 20 years of professional selling, I have seen thousands of mediocre salespeople with those traits. The number one trait of top selling, award-winning salespeople is organization! They simply do more and make more sales.

Imagine two outside salespeople. They have identical inventories and similar territories. They both work eight full hours a day. Salesperson Number 1 organizes his work to make ten productive sales calls each day. Salesperson Number 2 is not as organized and only makes eight productive sales calls a day. Who sells more? If everything else is equal, the organized salesperson will sell more, earn more money and win more sales awards. He should. He is making two additional productive sales calls per day. That is 10 more per week, over 40 more per month, and over 500 each year! That is the power of organization.

You can put organization to work for you, but it does not work free. It costs you a little of your time and effort. Consider Salesperson 1 and 2 again. Salesperson 2 rushes out to make as many sales calls as he can. He starts early, and works the whole time. That is good, but most of his time he wastes as he rushes from place to place trying to find a decision-maker willing to talk with him. On the other hand, Salesperson 1 takes a half an hour to think through his day. He plans the best way to work his territory, and he makes appointments in advance. That way, he can speak with more decision-makers. It does not matter when Salesperson Number 1 invests his time organizing. It can be at night, in the morning or at lunchtime. The payoff, however, comes all day long as he spends more time selling and less time waiting.

It makes sense that an organized outside salesperson can make more sales presentations and sales. Can organization help inside salespeople? It definitely does! Salespeople A and B both work in a department store. They work in the same department, and they both see the same number of customers each day. Why would salesperson A consistently sell much more than salesperson B? The answer to that question is organization!

Salesperson A invests a little time each day to review her inventory and prices to see what is on sale. She can answer any question from a customer, and she can quickly help anyone find the item he or she wants to buy. Salesperson B is the opposite. She invests no time organizing. She fumbles around trying to find the answer to any question from a customer. She cannot quickly find items from the inventory that her customer might want. Customers get frustrated with her poor service, and they leave without buying.

Organization also helps salespeople (inside or outside) sell more to each customer. Invest some time organizing your sales presentations. Know what you plan to say about your product in advance. Practice your presentation until you are comfortable with all the information. Be ready to answer any question from a customer. Organize in advance any samples or paperwork you need to make the sale so that you know just where they are. When you are well prepared, you can concentrate on what the customer is telling you. You can be more confident and more enthusiastic. That makes you more persuasive, and you sell more!

An important part of being organized is doing paperwork. Here are a few important words about paperwork. Every sales job requires some sort of paperwork, and nearly every salesperson would rather sell than fill out that paperwork. That is just the way we are! However, paperwork is not a four-letter word, and it is not your enemy.

As a young salesperson, I avoided paperwork, until I discovered this valuable selling truth: Paperwork works for you, not the other way around.

Here is the value of paperwork for any salesperson: First, **paperwork gets you paid**! If your sale is not processed and shipped correctly, then you will not get your reward for that sale. Second, **paperwork gets you promoted**. Managers do not spend much time with you as a salesperson. Managers do spend a lot of time with your paperwork.

Think of paperwork as your ambassador to management. No matter how much you sell, your managers, all the way to the top, regularly see your paperwork, not you. Either your paperwork impresses them with accuracy, neatness and timeliness, or it does not. Which salespeople will the managers choose when a special opportunity or promotion becomes available? They usually consider salespeople who successfully sell and submit quality paperwork. The time you invest to submit accurate, neat and on-time paperwork is always worthwhile!

The ability to concentrate and to use time well is everything.

*– Lee Iacocca, Philanthropist, author
and former automobile industry executive*

Etiquette Essentials
Support Your Boss

Following instructions and quickly doing what your boss asks you to do are two very important aspects of success. Your boss represents your company, and it is his/her job to ask you to do things that will benefit the company. Your boss expects your obedience. Learn to take direction well. You make your boss's life easier by being dependable. That does not mean you are a robot. It means you can be trusted to do important work. If you have questions about any task your boss assigns you, it is your job to ask questions. Just be respectful in when and how you ask the questions, and do not embarrass your boss in front of others. While doing that might seem funny at the time, it will come back to harm you later. Your boss will work hard to help you make a living and a good career, if you work hard to help your boss and your company succeed.

 is for Price

The price is right only on TV game shows.
For customers, it always starts too high.

Price is what a customer agrees to pay for your product. Prices can be negotiable or locked-in. An example of locked-in pricing is a snack vending machine. The price shows under the snack, and you buy it or not. Negotiable pricing, on the other hand, allows the seller and the customer to agree on a best price like when someone buys a house.

Every price is too high for every customer in the beginning of every sale. Consider that vending machine. People walk by it all day long without purchasing a snack because the price is too high for people who are not hungry. When someone gets hungry enough, suddenly the price is right. Then they buy from the machine.

All sales work the same way. Until customers believe that the product has enough value, they will not want it. When they do not want it, every price is too high. The main job of salespeople is to convince customers that the product has enough value to be worth the price. A sale happens when the customer agrees that the price is not too high.

The sale price can be very high if the customer wants the product enough. If the customer's want for the product is low, the price must be low to make the sale. Real estate provides some great examples. Hundreds of people can look at the same house, and only a few will want it at the selling price. Normally, when people do want the house enough, they make a serious, but low offer to buy it. The seller can accept that offer or come back with a price that is lower than the original but higher than the buyer's offer. This is negotiation, and it goes back and forth until the buyer and seller agree on a price. Then the house sells.

A different example is a gas station. The gas station owner wants to sell gasoline, so he opens his station and turns on his pumps. He puts up signs to attract customers who are driving by. Customers drive by, and the ones who agree that his price is acceptable will stop. They turn in and fill up their tanks. The gasoline sells, and the gas station owner makes a profit on the sale.

What is a profit? Profit is the money a business (or private seller) makes when something is sold for more than it cost to buy it or make it. People sell things to make a profit. In the real estate example, the seller made a profit if the selling price was more than what he paid for the house plus any expenses of selling it. No law says you must sell your product for a profit. Companies however must make profits; otherwise they run out of money and go out of business. No law says customers must pay any price that a seller asks. The higher your price, the more value you must show; otherwise, no customers will pay such a high price for what you are selling.

There are two kinds of prices: Asking and selling. The asking price is how much money the seller wants to receive for the product. The selling price is the amount of money a customer will actually pay for the product. The greater the value and cost of a product, the more a seller will usually need to consider reducing the asking price to make the sale. In business, coming to an agreement between the asking price and selling price is known as negotiation or bargaining.

Sellers and buyers negotiate to agree on a price. Here is an example of a basic negotiation: Randy has a car for sale. His asking price is $12,000. A buyer offers Randy $10,000 for the car. Randy says no and counter-offers $11,500. The buyer wants the car, and counter-offers $10,500. Randy wants to sell the car, so he counters with $11,000. The buyer agrees, and they have a deal.

Negotiating is an art. If you want to be good at negotiating, read books, study and practice. With study and practice, anyone can learn to be a skilled negotiator.

Etiquette Essentials
Maintain a Positive Outlook

A positive outlook on life is a valuable asset to you. To succeed in business, you must get along well with other people. Occasionally, some people with negative attitudes achieve some success, but other people dislike them and do not respect them. Remember Scrooge?

Positive people go through life expecting good things to happen. Positive people attract other people. Positive people make it through difficult times with less stress than negative people. Positive people are happy with themselves and others. Positive people find things to laugh about, and they laugh! Positive people are more fun. Positive people sell more!

Maintaining a positive outlook works like maintaining enthusiasm. Review the chapter on enthusiasm if you need to refresh your memory. If you want to be a positive person, start hanging out with positive people. Read positive books, watch positive TV shows, and listen to positive music. Stop exposing yourself to negative people and entertainment. Give up negative forms of speech, like sarcasm and gossip.

Positive people do not take other people for granted. Practice being positive toward others by using the words "please" and "thank you" as often as you can. When you include the words please and thank you in your conversations, voice mails, e-mail messages and letters, you show respect and consideration for your customers. If everything else is the same, customers will buy from the salespeople who show them more respect and consideration. It makes no sense to lose sales and income over such small things as neglecting to tell your customers "please" and "thank you." It happens! Make it a habit to use great manners with all of your customers.

I am not trying to turn you into a sweet little mild-mannered goody-goody. Being positive does not equal goofy. You can be savvy and very positive at the same time. Simply focus on how things can be achieved and how you and those around you can succeed. Leave your negative thoughts, negative talk, and fears behind. It will take some practice, but you can become a very happy, positive and successful person if you try.

A Different Perspective: An American Disadvantage

Americans are at a distinct disadvantage to citizens of other countries where bargaining is the norm. In much of the world, consumers bargain for their everyday purchases. In markets all over the world, the seller expects a buyer to bargain for a lower price. Americans evolved from bargaining into the "supermarket mentality." That means the price marked on a product is final. In supermarkets, the seller is all-powerful, and the buyer must "take it or leave it."

Sellers get away with this business model because buyers have enough money, but not enough time. Americans will pay more for variety and convenience. The supermarket system fits our fast-paced, affluent lifestyle, but it kills our negotiating skills. Americans are very experienced as buyers, but not as sellers

Most Americans stress-out when they see themselves placed in a selling situation because they are not experienced selling or negotiating. This is really just a perception problem because most of us "sell" everyday. "Selling" is simply persuading others that your idea has value. If everyone understood the essential concepts of selling, they could avoid much of that stress and enjoy selling!

Adding the polish builds profits. You will get the price you are asking if you understand the art of kindness.

– Edie Hand

 **is for Questions**

Questions are the keys that unlock sales.

All sales begin with customers thinking "no." It is up to salespeople to move customers' thinking toward "yes." Only customers know exactly what they want. (Sometimes they are not entirely certain.) Questions are the keys you use to open-up customers, to help them describe (and sometimes discover) what they want to buy. When you know what they want, you can show them how your product matches their description.

Questions are also tools you use to ask customers to buy your product or to give you more information. Like any tools, there are many types. You become skilled at using them by practicing with them.

There are two basic types of questions: short-answer questions and long-answer questions. The short-answer questions require just a word or two in answer: yes or no, a number, a color, etc. Salespeople use short answer questions to direct a customer's attention to a certain fact.

These are examples of short answer questions:

- Do you like cookies? (Yes or no.)
- How many cookies do you eat at once? (A number.)
- Would you like to buy two cookies or three?

Short-answer questions give the customer only a few options for an answer. Since you can be ready to respond to any of the possible short answers, short answers give you some control over conversations.

Long-answer questions open-up the conversation. Long-answer questions give the customer permission to talk more and to share their thoughts. You use long-answer questions to get information that helps you join the customer's world and discover what the customer wants. Examples:

- What do you like about cookies?
- What is good about your favorite cookie?
- Why do you think people love cookies?

As you have already guessed, the point of all of the previous example questions is to sell cookies. No matter what you are selling, be prepared to listen carefully after you ask a question. The information the customer gives you is like gold. It is valuable insight into what the customer believes. Once you know more about what your customer believes and wants, then you can tell that customer how your product can really benefit them.

Customers will tell you exactly what they want to buy, if you give them the chance. Ask good questions to get them talking. If the customer talks fifty percent of the time and you talk fifty percent of the time, then you have a fifty percent chance of making the sale. If they talk seventy-five percent of the time, then you have an even better chance of making the sale! On the other hand, if you talk one hundred percent of the time, your chances of selling anything very likely go down to zero. (How can a customer say "yes" if you are doing all the talking?)

Why is this true? Customers care more about what they want to buy than what you want to sell. This idea is so important that I am going to repeat it again: Customers care more about what they want to buy than what you want to sell.

"Pushy" salespeople never let a customer say much, and customers do not like that. It makes them feel uncomfortable. On the other hand, what makes customers feel comfortable is the sound of their own voice. The more they talk and feel they are being listened to in a conversation with you, the more comfortable they will be with you. This makes them more likely to buy from you.

Learn to ask questions that keep the customer talking about what they want. You can easily fit your product benefits into the two-way conversation. Customers enjoy talking to (and buying from) salespeople who always listen to their customers carefully.

You should ask one very important question in every sale. That question is some version of:

"Will you please buy this product from me today?"

It is your job as a salesperson to ask them for their business. It is your job as a salesperson to close your presentation by asking them to buy your product today. That is why asking them to buy is called "closing" the sale. Since not all customers say "yes," remember the lessons explained in "Chapter N is for No." If you ask customers to buy from you today and they say "no," then immediately ask them, "Why?" Otherwise, you may never know their reason. All customers are different, so there may be any number of reasons for not buying today. If many customers tell you the same reason for not buying, then perhaps there is something you can change and improve in your selling to get more sales.

If you do not specifically ask every customer to buy from you today, you will miss many sales. Customers might love your product but decide to buy it from someone else. They might agree that they want what you are selling, but just not right now. To sell effectively, specifically ask each customer to buy what you are selling. It makes sense to close each sales presentation by asking for their business. Here are some poor, good and better examples of how to ask customers to buy your product. First, some poor examples:

- You don't want to buy any _____ today, do you?
- (Of course, they don't if you ask like that.)
- So, what do you think? (About what?)

Here are some good examples:

- Would you please buy one of these today?
- Do you want to buy one now?

Here are some better examples:

- Shall I order one of these for you now?
- Which one of these ___ will you buy today?
- How would you like to pay for these today?
- Would you like to buy this one, or that one?

Your closing question should always make it convenient for the customer to buy from you. Offering customers a choice is a good way to make the customer feel like they are in charge of the sale. Instead of asking if the customer wants to buy, ask the customer if they want to buy this one or that one, A or B, chocolate or vanilla, etc. They get a choice, and you make a sale!

Another important question to ask is, "How will you be paying for this today?" The sale really is not over until the customer has paid you. Keep that in mind. Do not spend your valuable time selling to customers who cannot or will not pay you the correct amount when they should. In many sales, customers order your product and agree to pay you later. Never be embarrassed or afraid to go back to that customer to collect your money. Asking a customer to pay what they owe is basic business, and the customer expects you to call on them to collect. In fact, most customers simply wait to pay until the salesperson calls to collect.

You are doing them a favor by reminding them what they owe. When you call them to collect, smile and simply say that you need to get their payment for the last order. These days, most businesses will quickly give you a credit card number, a check or cash to pay for their order.

Always respect your customers by asking them directly if they would like to buy your product or service. They deserve that respect because they are giving you something valuable. At the same time, when you give them something valuable in return, you make a sale and you are helping the economy of your city, county, state, country and the world! Be proud to ask them to buy your product.

Another excellent question to use on every sales call is, "Do you know of anyone else who might want to buy one of these?" This question is asking for a "referral." Referrals are recommendations of other people who might buy your product. Referrals are usually very good sales leads. Your customer will have a good idea of who might really want your product. In addition, when you can tell the referral that your customer sent you, you have credibility. You can also ask your colleagues, friends and family-members for referrals! Asking for referrals is the best way to find new customers. It takes you two seconds to ask a question, and it saves you hours of prospecting to find another new possible customer.

Etiquette Essentials
Question Everything

Question everything. In other words, check and double check! We do not live in a perfect world. People make mistakes, and there are bad guys out there. Trust people, but verify that they are doing what they told you they would do. Confirm orders are correct and shipments are on time. Verify facts and details.

With new customers, have a credit check done before you open a new account for them. Get your business agreements in writing before you do a deal. Trust yourself first and be trustworthy to others. Then you can give other people the opportunities they need to win your trust in them. In life, like in business, you get what you inspect, not what you expect. You can be a positive person that expects good results and keeps your eyes open for problems at the same time.

Trust, but verify.

– Ronald Regan, 40th President of the United States

 **is for Relationships**

People like to do business with their friends.

Good selling will produce a sale the first time. Good relationships will produce sales the second, third, and fourth times, etc. As you develop a good relationship with your customers, you will find it easier and easier to sell to them. If you fall into a bad relationship, it will be very difficult to sell them anything.

Relationships take shape over time, and it is the salesperson's job to begin the process. When you see your customers for the first time, expect them to hide behind a wall of indifference. Why should they care about you or what you have to sell? You cannot blame them. As we mentioned in "J is for Join," customers expect some salespeople to fake friendliness just long enough to take advantage of people. You will have to show them that you are different.

You show customers that you are different by using the three B's of good relationships: Be sincere. Be honest. Be there.

(1) Be sincere. Start good relationships by sincerely caring about your customers and helping them solve their problems. Customers can see right through fake sincerity, so you have to keep it real. Put what they want ahead of what you want to sell them, and they will respect you for your sincerity.

(2) Be honest. Honesty is the glue that holds relationships together. You must be completely honest with your customers. As customers learn that you are an honest and truthful salesperson, they will begin to trust you. Customers are always looking for a salesperson they can trust. After a while, customers will realize that they trust you, and that you care about their wants. That is the basis of a good relationship.

(3) Be there. Customers will feel comfortable with you when they believe they can depend upon you for good service. They need to know you will be there to help them when they call. You accomplish this by working a regular schedule. Let your customers know what hours you work. Give them your phone number and e-mail address so that they can contact you. Make yourself convenient to work with, and people will want to buy from you. Being there again and again when your customer needs you creates a strong and lasting relationship.

The best salespeople contact their customers on a regular basis, whether the customers need to buy something or not. The contacts you make in between your sales are valuable for relationship building. Each time you see your customers learn something new about them. As you get to know them better, they get to know you better and your relationship grows. Your customers will see that you do indeed care about them and their business. Many salespeople develop friendships with customers that last for years or even a lifetime.

Good strong relationships will overcome problems. That is important because all businesses have problems. Maybe a product delivery is late, or maybe your product is defective. If you have a good relationship with your customers, they will work with you as you solve those problems instead of buying from someone else.

Here is some great news: When competing salespeople try to cut into your sales by calling on your customer/friend, they will hit the same wall of indifference you experienced at first. You however, with your solid relationships with your customers, are now standing on top of that wall smiling down on all those other competing salespeople!

Etiquette Essentials
Give Respect

Respect flows in two directions, up and down. You should show the proper respect for your boss and the people in your company's management. They in turn should show respect for you. So, what exactly is respect?

Respect is acknowledging what a thing or person can do. We respect rattlesnakes because they can bite us and make us very sick. We respect doctors and nurses because they can heal us. Before we cross the street, we look both ways. Why? Because we respect what a speeding car would do to us if it hits us. We also pay higher and higher prices for tickets to concerts and sporting events. Why? Because we respect the rare and unique performances those entertainers and athletes deliver. In a nutshell, we show respect by giving something we have to someone else who deserves it.

We show respect by our actions. Upward respect for our supervisors means doing the work they ask us to do on time and with few mistakes. We also show respect when we speak positively about our work and do things that makes our company stronger. We show respect to our government when we pay taxes. We show respect to our customers by providing them excellent service at a good price. We show respect for our families by spending time with them and working to provide for them.

Also very important is respect for everyone else. People who work around us, our peers, receptionists, janitors, maintenance people, and the people we pass on the street all deserve our basic respect. What do you have to give those people? A smile and a quick, "Hello, how are you today?" Just a little respect, like that, can make another person happy.

Respect does indeed flow in two directions. The people that you respect are more likely to respect you.

A Different Perspective: Success is a social event.

Selling requires at least two people: A seller and a customer. Success in selling requires customers, and it usually requires many of them. Since people like to do business with their friends, decide right now that you will learn how to make friends and keep in contact with those friends.

They say in business, it is not who you know, but who knows you that matters. Start making as many friends in as many places as you can. These are not customers yet. Friends help you through losses and help you celebrate wins. Join groups, meet your neighbors, and invest some time making friends! There are many professional groups, church groups, civic groups, hobby groups, etc., that will always welcome new members. Visit some of these groups to see if you like the people there. There is no obligation to join if you are just visiting. You might make some friends.

Like many of the ABCs of selling, making friends is a topic about which there are thousands of books. It is a good investment of your time to study the art of making friends.

Here is a tip to help you quickly make new friends: Whenever you are in a social situation, like a business reception or at church, take the first step to meet someone. Walk up to someone you do not know, smile and say, "I have not met you yet. My name is _____, and I just wanted to say hello." Offering your hand for a handshake might leave you standing with your hand out (if the other person does not take it), so just smile and speak. You will be amazed at how many people will enter into a friendly conversation with you if you start it first.

Friends enrich your life in many areas besides business. When you build good relationships with people, your life is more interesting. You feel connected to your friends. They feel connected to you as well. Isolation is often associated with depression. A broad circle of friends keeps you mentally healthy. (And you can rely on them to tell you when you have spinach stuck in the front of your teeth!)

We should be aware of the magic contained in a name and realize that this single item is wholly and completely owned by the person with whom we are dealing... and nobody else.

– Dale Carnegie, world famous sales trainer and motivator

 # is for Service

Take care of your customers, and they'll take care of you!

Service is all the things you do for your customers before and after they do only one thing for you—buy your product. The amount of service you need to provide depends on how much your customer wants your product. If they absolutely must have your product, you may not need to provide as much service. Gas stations, for example, provide no service whatsoever. You need gas to be able to drive your car, so you buy gas and pump it yourself.

On the other hand, when customers buy things they want but do not absolutely need, service becomes important. Luxury items like fine jewelry, exclusive dining, high fashion clothing and expensive cars are good examples. Shoppers of luxury items demand good service, and they decide where to spend their large amounts of money based upon the quality and quantity of service they receive.

Before a sale happens, you can impress customers with how you professionally serve them. Customers appreciate a salesperson that sincerely cares about them. Customers appreciate salespeople who do not waste time, who know the answers to questions, and who can make the sale without mistakes in billing, delivery, etc. Just as important, customers appreciate a salesperson with a pleasant attitude and who seems very happy to provide service. Who would want to buy anything from a grump?

Some examples of after-the-sale service are free installation for kitchen appliances, free delivery for furniture, free gift-wrapping for presents, free maintenance for automobiles, free cleaning for jewelry, and free sharpening for knives. A guarantee is a form of service, and it is important to many customers. If the product breaks while it is guaranteed, then the customer expects the service of a quick repair.

The best way to provide excellent service for your customer is to keep asking yourself, "If I was the customer, how would I want to be treated?" If you are not certain about how to provide excellent service, ask other successful salespeople how they do it. Watch them and learn. As you imitate what they do for customers, you will see how your customers react. From that reaction, you will learn the best services you can provide to help your sales grow.

Here is a basic service anyone can do immediately: Thank your customers. Thank them for shopping with you whether they buy anything or not. Especially thank them when they buy something. Anyone spending his or her time and hard-earned money with you deserves a pleasant, sincere thank you. Do you agree?

Special Note to Readers:

Thank you for buying and reading this book! I appreciate you.

Regards,
Dale

If you do build a great experience, customers tell each other about that. Word of mouth is very powerful.

– Jeff Bezos, Founder of amazon.com

Etiquette Essentials
Keeping Secrets

Can you keep a secret? Employees of companies hear company secrets. The more responsibility you have in the company, the more confidential information you receive. Alert employees also hear personal information from their coworkers. You may also hear confidential information about your neighbors, friends, people with whom you attend church, etc. In most cases, keeping secrets gets you ahead in business. When your boss and coworkers see that you can be trusted to keep important information to yourself, they will reward you by trusting you with more information and more responsibilities. More responsibilities for more pay is a promotion!

Why would anyone share a secret with someone not supposed to hear it? People do it all the time for a short-term gain. Usually they do it to impress another person; but it really does not work. The fact is, you lose the respect of the other person. They now think of you, and rightly so, as a person who cannot be trusted to keep a secret. They will trust you less in the future. If you cannot be trusted to keep a secret, others may wonder, "How many other ways are you untrustworthy?" Do you see the similarities between gossiping and not keeping secrets? Gossiping and revealing secrets may seem exciting and fine at the moment, but they often result in damaging your reputation.

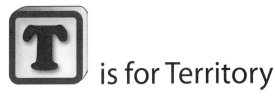 is for Territory

All your present and future customers together in one tidy package.

Territory is the term used to describe all of your customers and your potential customers. If you are an outside salesperson, your territory may be a zip code, or a city, or a state, or an entire country. An inside sales person might have one department in a store or maybe just one counter in a department as a territory. Regardless of the size of your territory, it consists of individual customers. As you know from reading this book, it is your job as a salesperson to join your customers' worlds, ask questions to identify what your customers want, share the benefits of your product so that your customers can see the value, and ultimately ask them to buy. Of course, you provide outstanding service before and after the sale to build a good relationship and sell them more later. See how these essential concepts fit together?

Organization is the key to making your territory a productive business. Being organized helps both outside salespeople and inside salespeople achieve more sales in a typical day of selling.

If you are an outside salesperson, learn where your customers are located and when may be the best times for them to see you. Plan how to see as many customers in a day as possible. Doesn't it make sense that if you can make more presentations in a day, then you will make more sales? Driving back and forth across a large territory will reduce the number of presentations you can make in a day. It is better to stay in one part of the territory all day instead of losing time driving back and forth. (I know of some salespeople who make sales calls with their cell phones while they are driving… I also know salespeople who have wrecked their cars while using cell phones! Please do not sell and drive at the same time.)

If you are an inside salesperson, better organization allows you to work with more customers each day. A telephone salesperson will make more calls per hour if he is well organized. Of course, the more calls you make the more you sell. Sales clerks in stores will be able to help more customers per hour if they know what merchandise is available to sell and where it is located. They will quickly direct customers to the products they want to buy, make the sale and move on to the next customer with a cheery, "Hello, how may I help you today?"

Manage your territory. Better yet, own it! Inside or out, large or small, always be looking for new business from your territory. Work every part of it, whether your territory includes three states or three counters in a store. If you are not assigned a specific territory, you are one lucky salesperson! If you can call on anyone anywhere to sell your products, the only thing holding you back is how much time you can work each day.

Etiquette Essentials
Telephone Manners Matter

Since cellular phones became available, we spend much more time on the phone. Here are some useful tips for making good professional impressions as you use the telephone for business...

At work, always answer your telephone professionally. Most people just pick up the phone and say, "Hello." Instead, to make a great first impression, answer the phone and smile. People can hear a smile in your voice on the phone, and they will listen more attentively! Say something like, "Good morning, this is Jane Smith. May I help you?" (You better get the time of day right! It's amazing how many people don't. Of course, be sure to use your own name.) With that little phrase, you make the person calling you feel comfortable that they have called the right person and that you are interested in helping them. You begin the conversation with a positive, professional tone, and the person on the other end will respect you for it.

Devote all your attention to the call. Customers can tell if you are checking e-mail messages, typing, driving, or other distracting things while you talk with them. Treat them like they are the most important person in the room or on the phone right now—because they are!

If you are the one who placed the call, you should be the one who says goodbye first. When the call is obviously over, end it politely by saying, "Thank you very much for speaking with me. Goodbye."

Do you know how you sound on the telephone? Try calling yourself from someone else's telephone, and leave this message: Tell yourself who you are. Then, ask yourself to go to your favorite grocery store and buy your favorite three items. Tell yourself where in the store the items are located and how much they cost. This exercise captures your voice as you ask someone to do something for you while you talk about something you know. That is, after all, what makes up most business calls. Later, listen to that message. Do you like what you hear? This is an easy way to hear how you sound to other people. If you need to make changes to how fast or slow you talk or to anything else, you will hear it in your message.

Be sure to end your message with, "Thank you." Thanking your customers is a very important part of business etiquette. Always remember that those customers could be spending their money with someone else. Tell your customers, "thank you," every time you have the chance. They will appreciate the fact that you are grateful for their business.

A Different Perspective: Sales... Hot, warm and cold

Outside sales is the opposite of inside sales. Clerks in stores wait for customers to come inside the store to buy. That is inside sales. Outside salespeople go to the customers instead of the customers coming to them.

In outside sales, a tip that a customer wants to buy something is a sales lead (pronounced leed). If that information will absolutely lead you to a sale, it is a hot lead. An example of a hot lead is a customer leaving a message wanting to place an order. A tip that might result in a sale is a warm lead. A customer calling for information about your product is a warm lead. A cold lead is really no tip at all.

A "sales call" is anytime you go see a customer in order to sell something. Most salespeople think of a sales call as a face-to-face visit with a customer. A telephone conversation is also a sales call, but it will not be as effective as a face-to-face-meeting. You cannot read the body language or the facial expressions of customers over the telephone.

There is another thing about telephone calls. Many customers find it easier to say no on the phone than in person. If you can make your selling presentation in person, be there.

Salespeople rate sales calls the same way as sales leads. If you already know a customer is going to buy, it is a hot call. If you can reasonably expect the customer to buy, it is a warm call. If you have not met the customer before and you do not even have an appointment, it is a cold call. Hot leads and calls result in more sales than warm ones. Warm leads and calls sell more than cold ones.

Cold-calling on new customers is one of the most enjoyable parts of any sales job, if you do it correctly. As you enter your customer's place of business, remember that you are in their world and on their time. Both are very valuable to the customer. The first thing you must do is introduce yourself to the first person you see. Explain who you are and what business you represent. Then you must give that person a great one-sentence reason to let you speak with the buyer. The first person you see is the "gate-keeper." The gate-keeper decides to let you see the person who can buy your product. Treat all gate-keepers with respect and patience as you wait to see the buyer. When you see the buyer, make a great first impression and start your sales call well.

Treat every customer as if they are your best customer and make them feel that meeting their needs is your top priority.

– Edie Hand

 is for Up-selling

Do you want fries with that?

Up-selling is asking a customer to buy just a little more. More what? More of whatever you are selling. The fast food industry made up-selling famous when someone very brilliant began asking everyone who ordered a hamburger, "Do you want fries with that?" To most customers, fries made sense with a hamburger, so they said, "Yes." Many hamburger places have had wonderful success up-selling fries and drinks. These days, before you even begin to order, many fast food places ask you if you want to try a combination meal.

Up-selling works well because your customers have already decided to buy. They believe that they can trust you and that your product has value. They are going to spend their money with you. What a perfect time to offer them something else they might want! This is one of the easiest ways to increase your total sale. All the customer needs to do is spend just a little more.

Here are some examples of good up-selling opportunities:

- a new shirt and tie when the customer has bought a business suit
- earrings with a new necklace
- a new belt with a new pair of pants
- new socks with new shoes
- an additional warranty with a new appliance
- popcorn when you go to see a movie

Speaking of movies, video rental stores have embraced the up-sell concept beautifully… When you check-out, you can buy candy, popcorn, gift cards, etc. They will also ask you if you want to buy damage-protection insurance for an additional twenty-five cents. What a great up-sell! It costs them nothing to ask you this question, yet by asking everyone they rake in thousands of quarters!

The key to successful up-selling is asking everyone. As soon as your customer agrees to buy your product or service, ask them, "Would you like _____ to go with that?" Many of the customers you ask will say no. Some of the customers you ask will say yes, however, and they will add significantly to your sales.

Etiquette Essentials
Understand and Be Understood

Misunderstandings happen wherever there is communication. What you think you just said may not be what the other person understood he heard. Put another way, in a conversation, people sometimes misunderstand what you mean. In business, that which you think you said is not as important as what the other person understood you to say. The same principle applies to your e-mail messages and letters.

It is our job to make certain that people we communicate with understand us. In a business conversation, it is perfectly acceptable to test the other person's understanding. Here is a polite way to do that: Say something like, "So, to test our understanding of what we just discussed, if I do ____, then you will do ____. Is that correct?" The other person can then agree or disagree. Making certain that other people understand you prevents mistakes, saves everyone valuable time, and makes you appear more professional.

It is also our job to make certain that <u>we understand other people</u>. Ask questions when you are having business discussions. Test your understanding of what the other person is saying. If they say something that is unclear, ask them immediately to go over it again. You can say something as simple as, "What was that again?" Never leave a conversation without fully understanding what the other person was trying to tell you. The other person will notice how you participate in the conversation, and they may ask questions to test your understanding. They will also appreciate how much you care about them and their business.

A Different Perspective: The champion of up-selling!

One of the most famous examples of a successful up-sell is from American history.

In April 1803, President Thomas Jefferson of the new United States of America was trying to buy the Port of New Orleans from Emperor Napoleon Bonaparte of France. America needed to expand and wanted a seaport "back door." Jefferson sent James Monroe and Robert Livingston to see Napoleon to make the purchase. Jefferson was prepared to spend up to 10 million dollars for the Port of New Orleans.

At that time, Napoleon seriously needed cash. He did not need 530 million acres of American wilderness. Napoleon, in a flash of selling brilliance, planned what may be the biggest up-sell in history. Napoleon sold New Orleans to the Americans with one condition: They must accept a special deal. For just a little more, they could also buy all the land from New Orleans to (what is now) Canada! President Jefferson had not intended to buy so much land, but he agreed to pay three cents an acre, or fifteen million dollars, for all of "the Louisiana Purchase." In those days, that was not cheap, but it made sense to Thomas Jefferson to spend more and expand his country. Napoleon got the cash he needed all because he asked for the up-sell. That was one world-class up-sell, Napoleon!

Change the picture in your mind and your voice will help you to up-sell.

*– Zig Ziglar, World famous sales training expert
and best-selling author*

is for Value

One good thing is a benefit. The sum of all good things is the value.

As discussed in the chapter, B is for Benefits, a benefit is one good thing the customer believes your product or service can do for them. Value is the total worth of all the good things a customer believes your product will do for them. Customers come to believe in one benefit at a time adding to the value. When the value of what you are selling outweighs the price, the customer will buy.

The customer must believe in the benefit for it to be relevant. This is a very important principle in selling. Many products have disappeared into history because the customers stopped believing in the benefits of those products. Buggy whips are a great example. When automobiles became the way to travel, horse-drawn buggy sales nearly stopped. Buggy whip sales declined too. Not because whips failed to work, but because customers no longer believed they needed a buggy whip.

The sales scales on the following page demonstrate how every sale works. The first sales scale shows how, at the beginning of any sale, the price always outweighs the value in the customer's mind. Before any sale happens, the customer must begin to believe in the benefits of your product. As benefits add up, the value outweighs the price and the scale tips. Ultimately, the sale happens. Yet, as you learned in the price chapter, every price is initially too much.

With the scale tipped toward No, the customer does not believe the product has value. The price is too great. There is no way he/she will consider buying it.

This is the normal state of mind for a customer who has no need for or does not want this product now.

When, however, the customer develops a need or begins to want the product, then the value begins to outweigh the price. As the value increases, the sales scale will tip towards Yes. Now the customer is in the Maybe state of mind.

Selling is persuading the customer that your product has enough value to outweigh the price. You add value by explaining one benefit at a time. When your customer believes that benefit, they move closer to saying yes and buying your product. When the benefits add up to enough value, the sales scale tips toward Yes, and the sale happens.

Want and benefits are closely related. The more benefits the customer believes your product has, the more your customer will want your product. The key to selling is explaining enough benefits so that the customer sees sufficient value to outweigh the price.

Sometimes customers believe in a product's value before they talk to a salesperson. Those customers are ready to buy right now. It is very important for you, the salesperson, to recognize that situation when it happens and make the sale immediately! You can easily talk customers out of buying. You might mention some issue that bothers the customer enough to stop the sale. That is like subtracting benefits from the value. If that ever happens to you, save your sale by adding more benefits. There is no need for you to continue selling once a customer says yes they are ready to buy. Close that sale quickly.

Etiquette Essentials
Voice mail and E-mail

Everyone knows what bad voice mail messages sound like… They ramble on and on and often leave out important information. They are sometimes funny as the person leaving the message stumbles and sputters and tries to get their thoughts together!

To always leave good voice mail messages, be prepared! What makes a good voice mail message? Another three B's: Be brief. Be bright. Be gone.

Make your voice mail messages brief. Busy people returning to their office after a day off or a vacation must slog through many voice mail messages. The last thing they want is long rambling messages. Organize your thoughts before you dial their phone number just in case you have to leave a message. It takes you less than a minute to prepare, and you are ready.

To leave a bright voice mail, leave this information: your name, your company, your phone number, why you called and your phone number. Did you notice the repeated phone number? Busy people with many voice mail messages often skim through them listening to the first few seconds to decide which one to call back first. They save the valuable ones and delete the junk. When they review their saved messages, it will be easy for them to call you back because your phone number is at the beginning. Repeating your number at the end is a courtesy and allows them to see if they wrote it down correctly the first time.

Here is an example of a good voice mail message: Remember to smile as you talk! "This is Dale Brakhage from the ABC's of Selling with Etiquette book. My number is 123-456-7891. Thank you for reading my book. Please recommend it to a friend or two. They will be very happy you showed them how to become more persuasive. Please call me if you have questions at 123-456-7891. Thank you!"

Have your thoughts organized ahead of time, so you can leave a bright, brief message. Then, be gone!

Business e-mail messages are very similar to voice mail messages. Bad ones ramble and are incomplete. Good ones are brief, bright, and short (because they are well-organized). There is no need to repeat your phone number in an e-mail message, but be certain to always include a phone number in case the customer needs to call you. For every e-mail message, take some time to write a good subject that lets the reader know your message is not junk mail (also known as SPAM).

Do not send SPAM. If you send frivolous e-mail messages that are not business-related, how will your customers know when you are serious? Reserve your business e-mail account for business e-mail messages. You will appear more professional.

A Different Perspective:
When ten percent can mean 1.3 trillion dollars!

"Selling" plays an important part in everyone's life. We "sell" other people on agreeing with our ideas in our daily conversations. Everybody sells. What is the difference between selling an idea and selling a product? There is no difference.

When you use the essential concepts of selling, your sales increase because you spend your time doing more of the important things that make sales happen. How much will your sales increase? Ten percent, two hundred percent or more? It all depends on how many of the basics you were using before.

Imagine how much stronger your company, or even the economy of our country, would be if all the salespeople suddenly became ten percent more effective. In 2008, the United States recorded a Gross National Product (GNP) of 13.8 trillion dollars. The GNP is essentially the total value of all goods and services produced by a country and sold on the market in a given period of time. If all the salespeople in the United States suddenly sold ten percent more, our gross national product would increase by 1.3 trillion dollars! That is a ten percent increase while a "good" increase is typically only three percent! That would be a tremendous boost to our economy!

A seasoned salesperson knows how powerful it is to deliver the gift of accomplishment to their customer. That is the power of the word Value. You show your value by walking your talk. You show a product's value by delivering its purpose with dependability.

– Edie Hand

 is for Want

Everybody wants something!

When a person decides in their mind that they should own something, they "want" it. Whether they buy it or not depends upon two things: The price and the value.

There are many different words to describe how much people are attracted to something. When we learn about something for the first time, we become aware of it. Then we consider it, and if we are attracted to that item, we like it. When the attraction grows strong enough that we are ready to take action to make it our own, then we want it. Wanting something is the first step toward buying it.

When people cannot live without something, they need it. People buy things they need without anyone asking them. They will shop around to find the best prices, but they buy food, gasoline, clothing and shelter whenever they need them. People just cannot do without the necessities. On the other hand, people buy the things they want when the time suits them and only when they believe the value they receive outweighs the price they must pay.

Wanting is often peer-reviewed. How does an attraction grow from something a person likes to something a person wants? It usually happens with encouragement from other people. When a person likes something, he may bring it up in conversation. The people in the conversation express their opinions about the product too. The group discusses the product and sets standards. If the group approves of the product, the person who brought it up becomes more attracted to it. (We take comfort in numbers.) On the other hand, if the group disapproves, the first person becomes less attracted to the product. Sometimes, very rarely, the group that approves of a product grows so large so quickly that a fad occurs. People have bought a lot of silly stuff because of the power of a fad. Do you still have a dusty skateboard somewhere that you cannot ride? I do!

One basic way advertising works is to show other people who want the product too. Commercials and print ads are full of smiling people who want a particular product. The message of those ads is this: "Be one of us! We are happy because we have this product!" Advertisers hope that someone who sees the ads will emotionally join the group and change from liking the product to wanting the product. As viewers of advertising, we then think, "Other people want the product, so it must be good."

To sell effectively, focus on what your customer wants. Ask questions to discover what they want. Then you can quickly show them how your product can fulfill that want. Do you see how important questions are to selling effectively? It is a shame that so many salespeople present their products without even asking what the customer wants. That is a waste of time. Since customers will quickly buy the things they want, then spend your valuable time asking what they want and explaining how your product does what they want.

In selling, the most important thing about your product is this: It is not important. **What is important in selling is what the customer wants to buy!**

Etiquette Essentials
Win with Class

When you apply these ABCs of sales and etiquette, you will sell more. You will win sales. Winning is wonderful! Enjoy it! Celebrate your success!

Keep in mind that the rest of the business world is watching you celebrate your win, so show some class. Act as if you have been there before. Thank the people who helped you win those sales. Give credit to the people who deserve it. Your customers and your co-workers will be happy for you, and they will help you win more sales in the future.

is for X-factor: Attitude

Believe you can: you will. Believe you can't: you won't.

[Warning: Attitude is an extremely powerful force. Do not operate attitude if you are taking medication or are under the influence of alcohol. Unexpected success can result from the proper use of attitude.]

People who understand attitude have a powerful advantage over those who do not. Attitude is an extremely important essential concept of selling. That is why there are many books available on the subject. This chapter teaches you how to make attitude work for you.

What exactly is attitude? Attitude is your inner feelings expressed in outer actions. If you feel happy inside, you begin to smile. If you are calm or angry, determined or confused, bold or frightened, etc., your face shows that too. The expression on your face is normally a good indicator of your attitude. The ways you sit, stand, walk, talk, dress, work or relax change with your attitude too. Typically, your behavior will reflect your attitude.

The fundamental purpose of attitude is to communicate your inner feelings nonverbally. Dogs are nature's best example of attitude. Anybody can immediately tell the difference between "happy, come and play" dog and "angry, stay away" dog. Of course, people are much more sophisticated than dogs. We can mask our inner feelings and we can adjust them. Later in this chapter, you will learn how to control and adjust your attitude. In any case, people around you judge if you are "safe" to approach based on your positive or negative attitude.

If your inner feelings and outward actions make you approachable, help you work well with others, and help you successfully accomplish your current responsibilities, then people will say you have a positive attitude. If your inner feelings and outward actions keep others away and keep you from success, then others will say you have a negative attitude. In sales, your success depends on customers who want to buy from you. A positive attitude makes you approachable and helpful, just the kind of salesperson customers want. A positive salesperson sells more.

Attitude affects all areas of your life, and it operates twenty-four hours a day. Only one person can manage your attitude: You! You can adjust it whenever you want if you understand how attitude works.

Here is the key to managing your attitude: Inner feelings affect outward actions directly and strongly; and that connection works both ways! If you change one, you affect the other. This is a very useful tool. It allows you to adjust your attitude from the outside.

The easiest way to change your inner feelings is to change your outer actions. Positive outer actions produce positive inner feelings. If you smile, you begin to feel happy. If you help somebody, you feel better for doing it. When you do something well, you feel better about yourself. Doing positive things gives you positive inner feelings. Positive inner feelings that in turn become positive outer actions are seen by the outside world as a positive attitude.

Which positive inner feelings can help you sell? Here are some I often use: Trustworthy, loyal, helpful, friendly, courteous, kind, obedient, cheerful, thrifty, brave, clean and reverent. ("Hello," to all the other Scouts who are reading this book.) The twelve positive attributes above are The Scout Law, and they are all positive. Of course, you can select any positive attributes you want to incorporate into your life. It does not matter where they come from. What matters is the quality of the positive attributes you choose to create inside of you.

Many successful salespeople live by the Golden Rule: Do unto others as you would have them do unto you.

Helping others is a wonderfully positive attribute for salespeople. It keeps them focused on what their customers want. The more positive inner feelings people have, the less room there will be for negative feelings.

Attitude is contagious! Strong attitudes affect weaker ones. Other people are naturally attracted to a happy person with a strong positive attitude. An angry person with a strong negative attitude repels people. Customers are always more likely to buy your product when you have a positive attitude.

When you start any sale, it is natural to feel unsure about yourself... You wonder whether or not the customer will say, "Yes." Will they buy? Everyone who has something to sell feels this way. Successful salespeople immediately answer those inner questions with a resounding, "Yes!" Unsuccessful salespeople think to themselves, "Maybe they won't buy. Maybe they'll say, 'No.'" You can think yourself out of a successful sale before you even contact your first customer. To prevent that, immediately replace any negative thoughts that enter your head with positive thoughts.

The "yes, they will buy from me" salespeople start earlier, make more sales calls and sell more. Those positive salespeople receive a wonderful "I won!" feeling every time their customers say, "Yes." That positive, victorious feeling boosts a positive attitude and gives the salesperson added confidence to sell more.

On the other hand, the "maybe they won't buy from me" salesperson will procrastinate. They will start later and make fewer calls. When a customer tells them, "no," it reinforces the salesperson's negative attitude. Then that negative salesperson believes, "I was right... No one is going to buy." Those negative inner feelings make the salesperson even more unsure and stressful. Other customers recognize that negative attitude and buy less. This process continues until it ends in complete failure. Avoid this situation! Start today to adjust your attitude and make it positive!

Always remember that inner feelings express outwardly. Customers easily detect attitudes. Your attitude affects the buyer's response to your selling proposal. This can work for you or against you. A buyer may say yes to a bumbling, positive salesperson. A buyer may say no to a very polished negative salesperson. Routinely, customers will avoid salespeople with bad attitudes and look for salespeople with good attitudes.

Here is a brief example: Occasionally, you must buy things you need (like gasoline or groceries) from a checkout clerk with a bad attitude. They make it obvious that they do not care about you. They do not want to be there and they do not care if you shop there. You just hate to give them your business! If you can avoid shopping there in the future, you probably do.

On the other hand, you enjoy buying the same items from a pleasant happy-to-help sales clerk. With everything else the same, the bad attitude clerk makes you want to shop somewhere else, and the good attitude clerk makes you want to shop there again. Keep this in mind when you are the one selling. Customers respond to your attitude. Keep it positive and sell more!

In closing about attitude, consider that a glass filled half-way with water demonstrates different attitudes… People who think the glass is half-<u>full</u> are **optimists**. People who think it is half-<u>empty</u> are **pessimists**. There is a third attitude, a very dangerous one… Some people think, "Who <u>stole</u> half of my water?" They are **victims**. The "victim attitude" is very dangerous because it blames others for bad situations. Who can ever expect to win if they believe that someone else is holding them back? To succeed in life, lose the victim attitude. Take personal responsibility for your situation, and do something positive to start making it better. With every positive action you take, your situation will get better and your attitude will improve too!

Etiquette Essentials
Good Manners is also an Attitude!

In etiquette, the X-factor is also attitude. Customers are attracted to well-mannered salespeople with positive attitudes. Good manners plus a positive attitude is a powerful combination. Good manners is a choice just like having a positive attitude is a choice. Work to improve yourself, practice etiquette, and develop a winning positive attitude. You, and the people around you, will be grateful you did!

The person who succeeds is the one who, step-by-step, views the end of the road with optimism.

– Edie Hand

 is for Yes

The most beautiful word in the world!

"YES" is the word salespeople work to hear. "Yes" means the customer agrees. "Yes" means that your product is "sold!" (Of course, we know the deal is never really over until you have their money.)

Customers usually tell you they like your product before actually saying, "Yes, I will that buy that today." These little signs of agreement show you that the customer is moving toward buying. Salespeople look for these buying signs along the way to a sale. The more buying signs you see, the closer you are to making the sale.

Statements like these indicate your customer's interest:

> "That sounds good."
> "Tell me more about that."
> "I have always wanted one of those."

Buying signs can also be in the form of questions. Serious questions like these tell you the customer is indeed interested in your product or service.

> "How much does that cost?"
> "Does it come with any options?"
> "Can I get it in yellow?" (Or any other color, size, etc.)

As the salesperson, you can sell more by always responding to a customer's "yes" with some positive statement. Make customers feel good about what they just said. Psychologists call this positive reinforcement. Reinforce every buying sign. Make the customers comfortable with the little steps they are taking toward the sale. If a customer says, "That is a great color," you reinforce with something like, "You're right," or, "Many of our customers think so." A small reinforcement keeps the sale rolling. If you go overboard with too much however, then the customer will think you are pushing too hard for the sale. This technique works best when it is casual and simple.

When you hear a customer say the first buying sign, prepare to ask them to buy your product. If the first buying sign is a very strong one like, "I love this!" then go ahead and close the deal by asking them to buy. They may say, "Yes." If they do not say, "Yes," right away, then continue to explain another benefit until they say another buying sign. Ask them to buy again. Give all customers the opportunity to say yes after they have given you two buying signs. (Keep in mind that many customers say no. That is fine. When that happens you immediately ask why, and keep the conversation going. You will have a chance to overcome their reason for saying no by adding more benefits.) When they believe the value of your product is worth more than the price, they will say yes and they will buy. This formula works. Either the customer says, "Yes," or they end the conversation before you can show them enough value to make the sale.

Be ready to show customers plenty of benefits. The more a product costs, the more a customer expects you to work for the sale. It makes sense that someone spending one thousand dollars should expect more attention than someone spending ten dollars.

If you want your buyers to say, "Yes," you must give them just enough information to outweigh their, "No." Give them too little, and they will not buy. Give them too much, and they will not buy. The trick is giving them just enough information. Here is an example:

A customer walks into a store to buy a new television. He asks the first salesperson he sees for some help. "The TVs are over there," says the first salesman as he walks away to take his morning coffee break. The customer does not buy from him. (Duh!)

The second salesperson is in the TV section. She makes a wonderful first impression by greeting the customer immediately and asking if she can help him buy a TV. "Yes, please," he replies. For the next thirty-five minutes, he follows her around the TV department looking at every TV and learning everything there is to know about modern television. The salesperson enjoys teaching people about TVs, and the customer is enjoying leaning about it all. Suddenly, he looks at his watch and exclaims, "I have to be at an appointment in two minutes! I am so sorry, I completely lost track of time. All I really wanted was a small color TV to go in my kitchen." Then he literally runs out of the store.

The second salesperson may or may not get that sale. She hopes the customer will come back later. If only she had asked questions at first, to discover what the customer wanted! Without that information, she treated a $400-customer as if he was a $4,000-customer. She ended up with a $0-customer. Lesson: Always be ready to take "yes" for an answer.

Etiquette Essentials
Say, "Yes," whenever you can.

Customers want to hear you say "yes." They come to you wanting a product or service. They want to find someone they can trust who will take care of their business. They are willing to pay a fair price to the right salesperson.

As you learn and apply these ABCs of selling and etiquette, you will discover yourself finding more ways to help customers get what they want to buy. You will discover more ways to match the benefits of your products and services to their wants. You will be able to say more and more often, "Yes, I can help you with that." As you say "yes" more often, you will become more persuasive, more successful and a much better salesperson.

> **Start with Yes even if you work your way back to No, because eventually there will be a Yes down the road.**
>
> *– Buddy Killen, Famous country music record producer and music publisher*

A Different Perspective: Bought and SOLD!

Even though only a small percentage of people are professional salespeople, nearly everything around us has been sold and purchased at least once.

Really, think about this for a minute… We pay for our food. We pay for a place to live, water to drink and sewer service. We pay for lights and electricity. We pay for heating and cooling. Someone, at some time, has paid for every acre of land in the United States. That means all the trees, flowers and animals on that land sold at least once.

Selling can be as simple as a can of beans sitting on a grocery store shelf with a price sticker on it. Selling can be as complicated as a multi-year bidding process involving major corporate contractors partnering to win a large government job. Most selling takes place somewhere in between.

It is hard to think of anything that has not sold at least once, and a salesperson is involved in every sale. Selling is definitely the engine that drives business. As a salesperson, you hold your future and the fate of your business in your hands.

Ideas are sold too. All the big ideas in the world started with one person. That person sold another person on it by explaining and persuading. Then the two of them persuaded others, and others, and others. How powerful is the ability to be persuasive? Ask Ghandi or Martin Luther King, Jr., or Donald Trump. It does not matter if you are building a social movement or a financial empire; knowing how to be persuasive—how to sell—will help you achieve your dreams.

 is for Zebra

Zebra? Yes. No kidding. Now, please pay attention. This last point is very important.

Imagine a herd of zebras stampeding across an African valley. Thousands of zebras are all running together, and it looks like a sea of stripes. One zebra, however, at the front of the herd, is completely black. Which zebra immediately captures your attention?

You notice the black zebra of course. Why? It is different. It has black stripes that are just a little wider than the other zebras. It has stripes that almost touch each other. That is what makes it appear black. It is still a zebra, not an elephant or a giraffe, so it can run with the herd. It is just a little more of a zebra than the rest. The black zebra automatically captures attention wherever it goes.

Now imagine a herd of salespeople all trying to get the attention of one buyer. There may be hundreds of them. How can one salesperson stand out from the crowd and capture the buyer's attention? By being the black zebra. All zebras have stripes, but the black zebra's stripes are just a little wider. All salespeople use some of these ABC's of selling, but some salespeople use more of them or use them better than other salespeople. All salespeople have manners, but some practice excellent etiquette. Excellent salespeople gain attention. That is why some salespeople seem to get all the sales. It is not magic, and it is not luck. It is because they are better at the ABCs of selling!

No matter what type of selling you do, you want to be the black zebra in the herd. You want the attention of the people you are trying to persuade. It does not matter if you are a politician stumping for votes, or a manager, or a coach building a team, or a parent or a teacher, you need other people to believe in the value of your ideas. You need to be more persuasive. You need those people to pay attention to you.

As you learn to apply the ABCs of selling and business etiquette, you will become more persuasive. People will be more likely to accept the value in your ideas. People will follow where you lead them. Buyers will appreciate you more than they do other salespeople. They will buy from you instead of others because you care more about what they want to buy instead of what you need to sell. Your managers will pay attention to you too as they notice your growing sales. Eventually, everyone will pay more attention to you as you become the black zebra!

Practice using at least one of the ABCs of selling every day. Practice at least one of the etiquette items as well. You will get better with them as you use them, and you will see positive results from other people. In twenty-six days, you will find yourself applying more and more of these in your selling. It will not happen overnight, and that is okay. You will see improvement happen over time. You can also refresh your new skills by occasionally re-reading and re-discovering chapters. The more you practice, the sooner you will see results. The more you practice, the wider your zebra stripes will become. Keep it up, be successful and enjoy selling more!

A word of caution to all you black zebras out there: Lions will notice you too, so you better keep running! When you are the black zebra, the top salesperson, you are the one everyone wants to beat. That is a great problem to have. It takes extra effort to stay the best, to stay out in front, but it is worth it. The view from the front of the herd is always better than the view from the back... The air is fresh, and the grass is green. When you are out in front in sales, the rewards and pay are much better! At the back of the herd, you eat dust and stare at the same old zebra rumps all day! Who wants to live like that? Not me, and I hope not you either.

Once you start applying these basic skills, your friends are going to notice. More and more, they will notice that you have persuaded them to do the things you want to do. When they ask you about it, it will be up to you to recommend this book. Go ahead. Why not help your friends become more persuasive and more successful too! They will be thankful that you did. Enjoy running at the front of the herd with your black zebra friends!

In closing

With knowledge comes great potential, with action comes great achievement.

Now you know. You know the ABCs of selling and etiquette. You know how to sell anything. You know how to be more persuasive. You know how to convince others of the value of your ideas. So what?

After reading this simple book, the fact is that you now know more about selling than most people.

The benefit of that fact is this: If you begin using these concepts, you can be more persuasive. You can sell more, you can earn more, and your customers will have greater respect for you. The key word here is if. Now it is up to you to take action. Go. Call. Visit. Write. Ask! You must contact a customer before any of these essential concepts can work for you.

Will you please start using these essential concepts of selling today? I have a strong feeling that you will. Good luck to you, and good selling!

About the book

During Dale's thirty years of success in sales, marketing, management and training, he used his training in educational psychology to observe and record the behaviors of award-winning salespeople. The results of his observations are the basis for this book. Educational Psychology is the study of human behavior as it applies to learning. Everyone learns differently and at different speeds. This book incorporates techniques to enhance learning. Readers of this book become engaged in a "conversation" with the authors. The style of the text is less formal and more accessible to attract and hold the attention of younger readers and those who communicate more frequently via the Internet. Selling is persuasive communication, a complex process. This book breaks the complex process of selling into simple behaviors that readers can easily learn and demonstrate. Those behaviors, called essential concepts, are presented in a matrix, the alphabet, which all readers can easily recall and recite correctly at any time. Associating the simple behaviors of selling with the alphabet provides readers with an effective memory device, called a trigger, which allows them to recall the behaviors easily.

About the authors

Growing up in Minden, Louisiana, *Dale Brakhage* was an Eagle Scout, lifeguard and an internationally competitive target shooter. He earned a summa cum laude degree in Educational Psychology in 1978. Entering the U.S. Army, Dale advanced to the rank of captain becoming a nuclear and chemical weapons expert. As if his life as a young man hadn't been eclectic enough, his professional career was just as notable... In the pharmaceutical, healthcare, e-commerce, and newspaper industries, Dale has excelled at sales, marketing, and sales team training and leadership achieving numerous notable sales and revenue-generation  milestones. Dale has worked with pharmaceutical giants Johnson & Johnson and Glaxo, managed marketing for LORTAB pain reliever as it become one of America's top-100 prescribed drugs, and later co-founded Scandipharm selling over a million dollars of new products in the first year and as Scandipharm's sales and marketing director helped grow annual sales to sixty-five million dollars. When Scandipharm sold, Dale moved on to lead sales and marketing in the e-commerce and newspaper industries. Formerly President of the Birmingham Chapter of the American Advertising Federation, today Dale is a regular contributor to national advertising web forums. He also serves as President of the Birmingham City Schools Career and Technical Education Advisory Board. He lives with Cora, his best friend and wife of 31 years, in Indian Springs Village, Alabama. They have two grown children, Athena and Erik, who live in Alabama. To contact Dale Brakhage, please visit his website at: www.DaleBrakhage.com

Edie Hand's philosophy for living life with gusto can be seen in everything she does from her work as an acclaimed celebrity chef, author, philanthropist, speaker, and business woman. Edie learned about the simple joys of family, life and helping others from her modest childhood growing up in the rural south. She is a cousin to the late Elvis Presley and also the cousin of 2007 Nashville Star winner, Angela Hacker. Edie recently co-authored *The Genuine Elvis*. She has authored, co-authored, and helped to develop over twenty books.  Edie has starred in national commercials and daytime television soaps. She has been the CEO of Hand N' Hand Advertising, Inc. since 1976. She is actively involved with American Women in Radio and Television and the National Speaker's Association. The Edie Hand Foundation works to benefit the Children's Hospital of Alabama, Children's Miracle Network, St. Jude Children's Research Hospital, and the Country Music Hall of Fame and Museum. For more information about Edie Hand, please visit these websites: www.ediehand.com and www.ediehandfoundation.org